Creative Grammar

Intermediate Level

W. Brian Altano
Bonnie MacDougall

Acknowledgements

The authors and publisher wish to thank the following people for their invaluable suggestions on the second edition of this text:

Lara Beninca, Academic ESL Instructor
Central Piedmont Community College
Charlotte, NC

Dennis Bricault, Director of ESL Programs
North Park University
Chicago, IL

Anne Bruehler, Instructor
Georgia Perimeter College, Lawrenceville
Atlanta, GA

Katherine Varchetto Grahl, Instructor
Henry Ford Community College
Dearborn, MI

Craig Machado, ESL Program Director
Norwalk Community College
Norwalk, CT

B. Nadine Nicholson, Instructor
Indiana State University
Terre Haute, IN

Ken Pakenham, Professor
University of Akron
Akron, OH

Charlene Polio, Associate Professor
Michigan State University
East Lansing, MI

Susan Salminen, ESL Program Coordinator
Raritan Valley Community College
Somerville, NJ

Linda Schrank, Professor
Rockland Community College
Suffern, NY

Frank Smith, Instructor
Georgia Perimeter College, Lawrenceville
Atlanta, GA

Karen Stanley, Academic ESL Instructor
Central Piedmont Community College
Charlotte, NC

Connie Ubben, Instructor
Johnson County Community College
Overland Park, KS

Lisa Wilkinson, Instructor
St. Louis Community College at Meramec
St. Louis, MO

Creative Grammar, Second Edition, High Intermediate Level

Produced and published by Spotlight Learning, an imprint of Real Media Solutions, LLC.

Publisher: Jacqueline Flamm
Associate Publisher: Paula Eacott
Editorial Director: Scott Cameron
Editor: Christy Newman, Weston Editorial
Cover and Interior Design: Robert Bovasso, Elizabeth Geary
Art: Brian Altano, James L. Barry
Principal Photography: Theo Solomon

978-0-9795523-1-1

First published 2005
Printed and bound in the United States of America 2 3 4 5 6 7 8 9 09 08 07

Spotlight Learning, an imprint of Real Media Solutions LLC

30 Cleary Avenue
Butler, NJ 07405

For information about Spotlight Learning, please visit our Web site at www.spotlightlearning.com.

Contents

units and topics

First Edition Acknowledgements

From W. Brian Altano

To Isabella: first and foremost, my friend; also, architect, painter, photographer, and poet, whose many skills have been usurped for these volumes.

To Brian, Daniel, and Erik, whose talents and personalities are disparate, but who have always shown me incredible loyalty and love.

To Azize, my assistant, whose critical eye and design skills have counterbalanced my computer illiteracy.

To Theo, whose photographs show the complexity of the human experience and the miserable joy that is life.

From Bonnie MacDougall

To my bewitchingly faceted husband, Donald Grein, and to my luminous, ardent daughter, Pia Twoney, who make my life enchanting to live.

To my ever-engaging students, who have taught me how to teach them.

To the English language, which I've been in love with ever since I figured out how to pronounce de-hu-mid-i-fier so many many years ago.

Second Edition Photo Credits

Introduction

To the Instructor

The intention of *Creative Grammar* is to empower students in their grammar-learning process and encourage them to use the points practiced in this book actively and confidently in their everyday lives. The approach supports the use of the four skills—reading, writing, speaking, and listening—in developing both fluent and accurate mastery of complex grammar topics.

With *Creative Grammar*, students read and look for specific constructions. They listen for grammar points. They write phrases, sentences, and paragraphs, focusing on what they have learned. Through guided conversations and communicative activities, students will practice speaking with many people: their instructor and fellow students, as well as their friends, relatives, and co-workers. When they speak, they will often do so with specific instructions concerning a particular tense, voice, or clausal construction. Instead of parroting grammar rules out of context, students will discuss how skillful speakers and writers use adjectives to add detail to their writing, present progressive to discuss future plans, and certain modals when they want to be more polite.

Creative Grammar is divided into 12 units of 16 pages each. Between the Grammar Introduction and the Unit Review, instructors are encouraged to take advantage of the flexibility built in to *Creative Grammar* and complete the activities in any appropriate order. An Answer Key allows students to use the book either in class or for independent study. Please note that the Answer Key pages are perforated so that they can be removed.

Within Level 2, students are still speaking and writing sentences, which are becoming more precise, detailed, and individual. To practice, master, and test the verb tenses, we use a mixed verb tense approach. Each tense is added to tenses we have already studied, and the emphasis is on recognizing time indicators that hint at which tense to use in verb cloze, sentence building, and sentence combining activities. Modals, noun and adjective phrases and clauses, and passive voice all follow on the heels of the verb tense study.

Each unit begins with a presentation of the main grammar point followed by a key capitalization, punctuation, or pronunciation point. Next, between 11 and 13 of the following activity types appear: Sentence Writing, Cloze, Writing Page, Error Correction, Theme-based Discussion (oral), Sentence Stems and Sentence Conclusions (completions), Grammar Discussion (oral), Communicative Activities (oral), Sentence Structure, Description of the Illustration or Description of the Photograph (written and oral), Grammar in Action, and Grammar Practice. The following is an overview of each activity type, as well as suggestions for classroom use.

Grammar Introduction Each unit opens with a presentation of the grammar point that introduces rules and provides many examples. Advise students to pay close attention to the sample sentences in order for them to understand the models. You may want to assign the grammar introduction as homework to be read in advance. That will allow you sufficient time to discuss how the grammar points are used in speaking and writing. These discussions usually spark greater interest in the concept.

Spelling, Punctuation, or Pronunciation The smaller, but key, points presented after the Grammar Introduction are often overlooked by students. They are, however, very important in developing oral and written fluency. Spelling is a particular problem for many English language students. Encourage them to learn the rules so that they can apply them outside of English class in their everyday lives.

Cloze Cloze activities require students to practice several different skills. They must understand vocabulary, tense, voice, and number. They are also a good test of whether students understand singular and plural nouns and subject–verb agreement. Finally, cloze activities provide practice in word positioning, the correct placement of words in the context of the sentence. Cloze activities work well as paired activities.

Sentence Writing Students write sentences on their own within specific scenarios. The production of sentences (rather than simple fill-ins) demonstrates an understanding and an active grasp of the grammar point. On occasion, have your students copy their sentences on the board for the class to check against the models. The atmosphere of the class becomes collaborative as students edit each other's work.

The Writing Page   This activity extends the **Sentence Writing** activity. In many cases, students are asked to write several sentences or a paragraph based on a specific theme. In writing and correcting this assignment, it is important to focus on the specific grammar point highlighted in the unit. Other grammar mistakes might be pointed out, but the goal is to provide practice on specific structures.

Error Correction   The mistakes presented in this section are common ones (such as the use of infinitives after modals or confusing present and past participles). It is sometimes easier to examine other people's mistakes, so this activity can serve as the focus of discussion.

Theme-based Discussion   The topics of the Theme-based Discussion are current and varied. The activity should begin in small groups and then expand to the entire class. It is essential for the instructor to monitor students' grammar, but not censor their ideas and opinions. The purpose of this activity is to encourage students to speak and listen, as they use the targeted grammar constructions accurately and appropriately. Theme-based discussions also assure students that what they are learning is not theoretical but practical.

Sentence Stems and **Sentence Conclusions**   In these activities, students complete the beginning or ending of sentences. This is a creative activity because there are so many correct answers. In addition, students have to understand whether the missing part of the sentence should be positive or negative. Stems are best done as an individual in-class activity or homework assignment. **Sentence Frame** activities contain both sentence stems and sentence conclusions.

Grammar Discussion   The Grammar Discussion point is introduced first in a text box in the Grammar Introduction section. Often it is an activity based on the grammar used in real life. The approach here is to have students question how common the grammar point is, whether it is used correctly or incorrectly most of the time, and what the specific uses of the point are. For example, it is interesting to discuss why the present progressive is used in police investigations. The study of grammar is a constant in most ESL students' lives. Making it come alive for them is essential.

Communicative Activities   These activities vary greatly and include surveys, interviews, games, map-making, and paired activities. They focus on the grammar point and encourage awareness of its use. Students are often inspired to become actively involved in language learning in these tasks.

Sentence Structures   Sentence structure practice concentrates on aspects of punctuation, word order, subject–verb agreement, and the sequence of tenses. All of these elements are combined in the activity, just as they would be in real-life English use.

Description of the Illustration or **Photograph**   Each unit presents illustrations or photographs, which serve as the basis for writing and discussion. Students analyze the illustration or photograph and compose sentences or paragraphs about it practicing the specific grammar point. There is generally a lot going on in the pictures, so encourage a class discussion for a few minutes before the students write. For further practice, you might have them cut out their own photographs, cartoons, or drawings, write about them for homework, and bring them to class for discussion and further work.

Grammar in Action   Grammar does not take place only in grammar class. Everything written is based on grammar (even if the grammar is incorrectly used, as in e-mail messages and some advertisements). This interactive section presents reading passages or interviews illustrating grammar points. The passages include newspaper and magazine articles, which are of interest to students, but whose primary purpose is to show that the grammar point is not used only in the textbook.

Grammar Practice   This section concentrates on traditional activities such as sentence combining and changing the tense according to time indicators. Students are quite familiar with this type of drill, which is best done for homework and then selectively corrected in class (going over only the odd-numbered sentences, for example).

Unit Review   Each unit ends with a Directed Writing activity that serves as a unit grammar review. Each writing assignment takes students step by step through a three-paragraph writing activity that encourages them to use the grammar of the unit in a specific, personal situation. Students are carefully guided through the writing process. In prewriting, students are asked a number of questions and given suggestions to help them make notes about the topic. For the first draft, students are given explicit instruction about how to use the grammar of the unit in their paragraph as well as guidance about main idea, details and conclusion statements. A first-draft model is also provided. For the revision, students exchange paragraphs with a partner who reads a series of questions to make sure all of the information has been included and the grammar is correct. Students are then assigned the final draft. Students have a list of criteria that you will use in the evaluation process.

We hope these materials assist you in making your grammar class one in which the following can be found:

- a high standard of grammatical accuracy in meaningful, relevant, significant sentences;
- a genuine curiosity on both your students' and your part about how various structures are used in different social settings;
- a playful environment where learners are encouraged to explore English and make their own discoveries. Mistakes are not to be feared but instead can serve as material to be examined;
- a welcoming, collaborative environment where students enhance their knowledge of English structure;
- a classroom environment where the issues of the day and the events of your students' real lives are respectfully brought into the learning experience;
- a set of strategies that students can develop in class and continue to use after finishing formal English study to deepen their understanding of how English grammar is used by real people for real purposes.

The goal of this text is to make the study of grammar more creative and enjoyable, allowing students free rein to their imaginations in writing and the chance to fully participate in a range of communicative activities. Enjoy yourself.

W. Brian Altano
Bonnie MacDougall
Originally written: Paramus, New Jersey 2005

Unit 1

The Present Tense: Simple and Progressive

When we talk about our habits, the things we do all the time, and when we describe people, places, and objects, we use the present tense. When we talk about our current situation, the way we live, think, and feel, we also use the present. There are two tenses that are used for these specific purposes: the simple present and the present progressive. Let's analyze them.

The Simple Present Tense

The keywords indicating the use of the simple present are: *every (every day, every month), each (each Saturday), on (on Thursdays), in (in the summer),* and adverbs of frequency *(always, sometimes, never,* etc.*).*

The simple present tense is used to express facts, personal habits, and cultural norms.
Harold **has** long hair and a moustache.
I never **eat** peaches, but I **love** apples.
Many people **watch** the news at 10 p.m.

Forming the Simple Present Tense

Affirmative and Negative Statements

Use the base form of the verb except for the third-person singular. For the third-person singular, add a final -*s* with regular verbs.

I **listen** to rap music on my way to work.
You **look** more beautiful every day.
Don **works** in the library every weekend.
Sheila **loves** peaches.

We **don't have** tennis practice on Wednesdays.
The two **vow** to never give up.
Our nations **face** difficulties.

Practice pronouncing the -*s* for third-person singular by "saying" the verb in your head. That kind of practice will help you remember the final -*s* when you are taking a test.

Also remember that the more complex texts you read, the more you may find complicated third-person singular sentences. Look at these phrases that mean *he, she,* and *it.*
he: **The long-suffering but gentle laboratory-created monster** baffles scientists.
she: **Charlie's intelligent, elegant bowling partner** charms everyone.
it: **The flow of air from west to east** causes weather patterns.

Yes/No and Information Questions and Short Answers

Are you awake?   **Yes, I am./No, I'm not.**
Is he home yet?   **Yes, he is./No, he's not. (No, he isn't.)**
Do they **have** a laptop?   Yes, they **do.**/No, they **don't.**

When do I **find out** my grades?   Next Thursday.
How many egg rolls **do** we **need** for the party?   One for each person.

The Present Progressive Tense

Present progressive tense is used in the following situations:

1. **to describe an action that is happening right now, at this moment**
   I'm sitting in the classroom now.   Mei **is looking** out the window.
   They **are not taking** notes.

2. **to describe an action that is in progress over a period of time (often with words such as *nowadays*, *these, today,* and *tonight*)**
   Are you **watching** the sci-fi marathon today?
   These days, Franco and Abdu **are working** at the restaurant.

3. **to talk about future plans**
   On Saturday, we **are having** a party.   I'm **writing** my paper next week.
   What **are** you **doing** at 4:00 tomorrow?

Forming the Present Progressive Tense

Affirmative and Negative Statements and Questions
Use *be (am, is, are)* + the present participle (base form of the verb + *-ing*). Contractions are commonly used with present progressive in statements.

I **am singing**.	We**'re** already **planning** Erica's wedding.
You **are crying**.	They**'re running** right now.
She **isn't studying**.	**Are** you **wearing** your contacts today?

Stative or Non-Progressive Verbs

Some verbs are not used in the present progressive, except as idioms.

1. **verbs of the senses**
   You **look** lovely. The wall **feels** rough.   This CD **sounds** awesome. This steak **tastes** great.
   Your soup **smells** delicious. I **see** you.

2. **verbs of emotion**
   I **love** you. Do you **like** me?   Sammy **fears** dogs. He **hates** cats.

3. **verbs of the mind or desires**
   My mother **forgets** everything. I **need** some rest now.   Ned **knows** all about cars. Nora **wants** a toy.

4. **verbs of possession**
   I **have** a Toyota. Mr. Bim **owns** three jets.   She doesn't **possess** an ounce of sense.

Present Progressive in Idioms

Many stative or non-progressive verbs are used in the present participle (be + base verb + *-ing*) in expressions and idioms. Consider the verbs *have, be,* and *see.*

have* vs. *be + having
Illness: He has a cold.
Family: They have a son.
Ownership: She has a BMW.

Experience: He is having a hard time in math.
Eating: They are having breakfast.
Drinking: She is having a soda.
Pregnancy: She is having a baby this month.
Hosting: They are having a party tonight.

see* vs. *be + seeing
Sight: I can see two pelicans.

Professional Appointment: I'm seeing Dr. Lee today.
Dating: Pia and Bill are seeing each other.

be* vs. *be + being
Existence: It's a boy!

Behavior: You are being mean.

Pronunciation of final -s

In simple present tense, the verbs for *he, she,* and *it* always end in *-s* or *-es*. Sometimes the final *-s* is pronounced /s/, and other times it is pronounced /z/. Its pronunciation depends on the final sound of the base verb.

The *-es* is usually pronounced /ɪz/.

Final Sound	Pronunciation	Verbs
all vowels and most consonants	/z/	s**ee**s, ann**oy**s, s**ue**s, be**g**s, ca**ll**s, s**ew**s
p, t, k, f	/s/	ho**p**s, si**t**s, tal**k**s, coug**h**s
s, z, sh, ch, soft g	/ɪz/	mess**es** up, los**es**, wash**es**, latch**es**, gaug**es**

◼ 1-1 Pronunciation

Look at the base form of each verb in the first column. Write the third-person singular present tense and then indicate its pronunciation by placing an **X** in the appropriate box. Practice saying each form correctly.

Base Form	Third-Person Singular Present	/s/	/z/	/ɪz/
stop	*stops*	X		
wait	*waits*			
miss				
sleep				
go				
read				
drive				
start				
pass				
love				
point				
type				
play				
watch				
want				
talk				
need				

◼ 1-2 Sentence Writing

Personal Habits

A. Use the simple present tense to write about three of your habits. Write both affirmative and negative sentences.

Example: I don't do homework until the last minute. I eat popcorn at the movies.

1. _____

2. _____

3. _____

Cultural Norms

B. Use the simple present tense to write about three ways in which your family celebrates your birthday. Write both affirmative and negative sentences.

Example: We usually go out to dinner for my birthday. I don't receive many presents.

4. _____

5. _____

6. _____

Stative Verbs

C. Use the simple present tense to write about three things that you can *see, hear, smell,* or *taste* right now. Write both affirmative and negative sentences.

Example: I see a few cars in the parking lot. I don't hear much noise.

7. _____

8. _____

9. _____

Current Activities

D. Use the present progressive tense to write about two activities you are doing right now, at this minute. Write two more sentences about things you are not doing right now.

Example: I am studying English now. I'm not eating lunch.

10. _____

11. _____

12. _____

13. _____

Plans in the Near Future

E. Use present progressive to write about four activities you are planning for this weekend. Write both affirmative and negative sentences.

Example: I'm not writing a paper this weekend. I'm going to the beach on Saturday.

14. _____

15. _____

16. _____

17. _____

Jean-Paul Sartre's book *The Other* is sometimes discussed in literature and philosophy classes. Who is "the other"? Look at the illustration. An alien (certainly a form of "the other") has come to Earth to talk with you. In groups of four, imagine that you need to explain "Earthling" behavior and customs to the alien.

A. Explain to the alien how people of Earth react to those who are different. What happens to people of Earth when they encounter "the other"? How do people of Earth react to differences in religion? What happens to people of Earth when they encounter differences in eye or skin color? Make the alien understand how and why we react to differences.

B. Explain marriage to the alien. Talk about who gets married, why people marry, and at what age they usually marry. Also, explain the customs surrounding marriage, such as the wedding. Why do people have weddings? What are some of the customs of weddings? Who, for example, pays for the wedding and why? Why does the bride wear a fancy dress, and why do her friends dress up on her wedding day? When you finish explaining marriage to the alien, explain divorce to him or her.

■ 1-4 Grammar Practice

A. Time Indicators are words that show which tense to use. They can appear alone, in phrases, or in clauses. With a partner, begin to develop a list of such time indicators that are used with the simple present and the present progressive tenses. Begin with the sentences in the unit introduction, continue with Activity 1-2, and fill in the two columns for the two tenses listed below.

	Simple Present	Present Progressive
Words	always	now
	_____	_____
	_____	_____
In phrases	<u>every</u> year	<u>these</u> days
	_____	_____
In clauses	<u>when</u> she gets up	<u>while</u> you are making noise
	_____	_____
	_____	_____
	_____	_____

B. Write a sentence with each time indicator.

always _____

every (day, week, month, year) _____

_____

when _____

_____

now _____

these days _____

while _____

_____

■ 1-5 Theme-based Discussion

Read each topic below. Make sure you understand the questions. Work in groups of four to discuss the first topic. Then choose one person to report the group's answers to the class. Next, move to another group to discuss the next topic. Repeat this process until all the topics are discussed.

A. There is no doubt that moviegoers are fascinated by superheroes. *Spider-Man* and *Spider-Man 2* are two of the most successful films of all time. Hollywood has made many Superman and Batman movies, along with X-Men, Catwoman, and the Incredible Hulk. There may be Wonder Woman and Iron Man. What do you think of superhero movies? Why do you think they are so popular?

B. Which superhero would you most like to be? Why?

C. With your group, create a new superhero. What is your hero's name? What does your hero look like? What can he/she do? Why does your hero fight crime? Share your group's information with the class.

■ 1-6 Sentence Analysis

Work with a partner. For each sentence, decide which tense is appropriate—simple present or present progressive. Also choose either the affirmative or negative form of the verb. Fill in the blanks with the correct form of the tense you choose. When you are finished, share your choices with the class. Be prepared to explain your reasons.

1. Mia's toe is broken, so she _____*doesn't walk*_____ (**walk**) much these days.

2. Ginann _____ (**drive**) her mother's car to work this month.

3. Joan's husband _____ (**work**) late most evenings.

4. Her cousin _____ (**have**) two cars and three bicycles.

5. He lost his pen, so he _____ (**use**) a pencil until he finds his pen.

6. Lola _____ (**have**) a headache almost every day.

7. Ahmed _____ (**study**) for each test, so he usually gets good grades.

8. We always _____ (**need**) extra sleep.

9. They _____ (**wash**) their dishes by hand because they do not have a dishwasher.

10. There is a problem with Min's car, so she _____ (**take**) a bus.

11. My brother _____ (**work**) at a radio station in Cleveland.

12. Please be quiet. While you are making noise, I _____ (**think**) about my term paper.

13. The Kims _____ (**have**) a good time at the beach this week.

14. Ona _____ (**study**) for the test tomorrow.

15. Mehmet _____ (**prefer**) to nap in the afternoon.

16. Amisi _____ (**wear**) a blue dress.

17. Mauricio _____ (**know**) a lot about science.

18. Rosa _____ (**like**) a cup of tea when she gets up.

■ 1-7 Communicative Activity

A. With a partner, talk about the photograph. What are these people doing? Are they on vacation? Do you think what they are doing is fun? Use simple present and present progressive to write at least five sentences in your notebook.

B. Compare your sentences from Exercise A with another pair. Do you have the same opinion?

C. Ask at least three students about what they do for fun. For example, do they walk in the park or go dancing? What don't they do? In your notebook, write sentences about their preferences. Share your sentences with the class.

Example: Shinu walks in the park. She doesn't run. Tajmah rides her bicycle. She doesn't watch TV.

1-8 Grammar in Action

A. Why do some people hate to fly? Write a paragraph giving three reasons why people hate to fly. Use this structure:

Topic sentence: There are three main reasons why people hate to fly.
The first reason is that ... (Write a fact or your opinion. Give examples.)
Another reason is that ... (Write a fact or your opinion. Give examples.)
A third reason is that ... (Write a fact or your opinion. Give examples.)

_____

_____

_____

_____

_____

_____

_____

_____

_____

_____

B. Think about a place that you love. Sit quietly and let this place surround you. In your notebook, describe what you see, hear, smell, and feel there. Describe it so well that everyone else will love it as much as you do.

C. Does someone get on your nerves? What is this person doing that bothers you so much?
Begin with: _____ is getting on my nerves these days because _____.
Write a full paragraph in your notebook, describing what this person is doing to annoy, irritate, and bother you. Use the space below for notes.

Notes

■ 1-9 Error Correction

Read the sentences below. Each sentence has at least one mistake. The mistakes could be in subject–verb agreement, simple present vs. present progressive, or missing words. Underline all the mistakes in each sentence. Then write the sentence correctly.

1. John has a party this Saturday night.

   John is having a party this Saturday night.

2. Bruce and Bob are loving to playing chess. They very good player.

   _____

3. Do you wanting go to a club with me on tomorrow night?

   _____

4. Marco don't want to go to his mother-in-law's house, but he going anyway.

   _____

5. Do you smelling burned bread? I am hating that smell.

   _____

6. Why you always yells at the dog? He just a animal.

   _____

7. I am always writing in my journal before I going to bed.

   _____

8. This fall, I am going to looking at the beautiful leaves.

   _____

9. I am not liking apple pie. It too sweet.

   _____

10. I am always listening to music when I cleaning the house.

    _____

11. When you leaving? Your brother going with you?

    _____

12. Right now, Paul living in Florida with his parents.

    _____

13. Quincy eat too much, so he very fat now.

    _____

■ 1-10 Sentence Stems

Use the sentence stems below to write statements using the simple present or present progressive tense. Write both affirmative and negative statements. Make sure the subjects and verbs agree and that you choose the appropriate tense.

1. Every Saturday afternoon, *my friends go to the game.* _____

2. This semester, _____

3. In the summer, _____

4. My sister's ex-husband _____

5. This Friday night, _____

6. Helga's two brothers _____

7. On Thursdays, _____

8. I don't like people who _____

9. After dinner every night, I _____

10. When I am very nervous, _____

■ 1-11 Sentence Conclusions

Use the sentence conclusions below to write true statements using the simple present or present progressive tense. Write affirmative and negative statements. Make sure the subjects and verbs agree and that you choose the appropriate tense.

1. _____ *I am usually sleeping* _____ at two o'clock in the morning.

2. _____ on Monday morning.

3. _____ whenever he gives her a gift.

4. _____ right now.

5. _____ whenever I feel depressed.

6. _____ every July.

7. _____ short, chubby and nice.

8. _____ a very large house and a BMW.

9. _____ long, black, and curly.

10. _____ very big feet.

■ 1-12 Description of the Photograph

Look at the photograph. Use it to complete the activities.

A. In your notebook, write a description of each of the two people in the photograph. What are they like? What do they like to do?

B. Now imagine their life at present. Where do they live? What are their lives like? What are they doing right now?

■ 1-13 The Writing Page

A mosaic, like the one below, is a complex piece of art. It uses many small, distinct elements to create a bigger picture. People are also very complex. You might say that we are like mosaics, composed of many tiny elements that make up our complicated selves. In one paragraph, write an accurate description of the way you are today. What are the key elements of your personality and your nature? Use the simple present and present progressive tenses.

_____

_____

_____

_____

_____

_____

_____

_____

1-14 Unit Review

Directed Writing

Task: Write a three-paragraph essay describing yourself.

Prewriting

When you meet new people (in a class, at a job interview, at a party), you need to introduce yourself. You answer questions, such as: What's your name? Where are you from? What do you like to do? What are you studying? What do you want to do when you graduate? In your notebook, make notes about yourself. Use a chart like the one below.

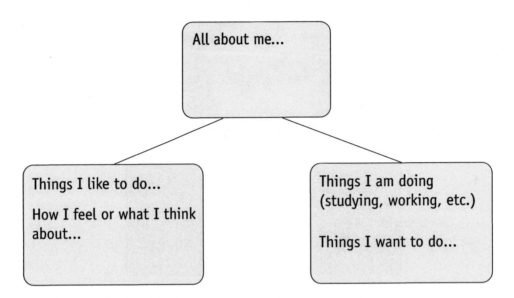

First Draft

Write a first draft of your essay. Use your chart and notes to organize your ideas as you write. Check that the first sentence of each paragraph states the main idea of the paragraph. Use simple present verbs to tell about who you are and what you like to do. Use present progressive verbs to tell about what you are currently doing in school, at work, or in your free time. Remember to indent the first line in each paragraph of your essay.

> **Model**   My name is Elena and I am from Guatemala. I am a quiet, shy person who loves to sing, play tennis, and...
>
> Music is very important to me. I listen to my iPod® all the time. My favorite type of music is...
>
> Currently, I am studying music theory in school. My dream is to be a composer. I am also taking some courses in...

Revision

Read through your essay and check for correct usage of the simple present and present progressive tenses, appropriate time indicators for the tenses, clear main idea and details, and correct spelling and punctuation. Share your essay with a partner. Your partner should be able to answer the following questions about your essay:

- Who are you? What are you like?
- What do you generally do? What do you like to do?
- What are you doing now in your life, and what do you want to do in the future?
- Did you use correct forms of the simple present and present progressive tenses?
- Do you have any errors in spelling or punctuation?
- Does the essay need any more information?

Final Draft

Make any changes or additions that are needed in your essay. Then write or type a final copy. You may want to include your final essay in a portfolio of your writing.

Evaluation

Your teacher will grade your essay. You will be evaluated on:

- clarity of main ideas and level of supporting detail in your essay;
- correct use and forms for simple present and present progressive; and
- use of appropriate time indicators for the simple present and present progressive.

Unit 2

The Past Tense: Simple and Progressive

Use the past tense to talk about time and events that are over. There are two primary past tenses: simple and progressive.

The Simple Past Tense: *It's History! It's Over, Done, and Gone!*

The simple past tense recounts national, cultural, and personal histories.

1. **The simple past tense is used to report actions or conditions that are completed.**
   The college **had** 2,500 students in 2002.
   My roommate **bought** a car a long time ago.

2. **The simple past is often used to report sequences of past actions—that is, actions that go in a specific order.**
   First, I **thawed** the steak. Then, I **cooked** it. (You cannot cook the steak and then thaw it.)
   We **studied** all week and **took** the test on Friday. (You don't study after a test.)

Forming the Simple Past Tense

Affirmative and Negative Statements
Many simple past verbs are regular. They form the past by adding -*ed*.
I **finished** my paper late last night.
Blimpie's® Sandwich Shop **opened** in 1964 and **closed** in 2002.
The team **needed** one more player for softball.
Some simple past verbs are irregular. You'll need to learn how the verb changes; for example, *go—went; have—had; get—got.*
Jane **went** to the concert with Syed.
We **had** a car accident two days ago.
I **got** a good grade on the test last week.
Look at the chart in the Appendix for a list of past forms of the most common irregular verbs. Using them often will help you memorize them.
Negatives in the simple past are regular: did not (didn't) + the base form of the verb.
I **didn't see** that new movie last night.
They **didn't receive** the check on time.

Yes/No and Information Questions and Short Answers
Questions in the simple past are formed with the past tense of *do* plus the base form of the verb.
Did she **go** to class yesterday? Yes, she **did.**/No, she **didn't.**
Did they **eat** dinner with you last night? Yes, they **did.**/No, they **didn't.**
Where **did** I **put** my keys? On the dresser.
Questions in the simple past with *be* do not use helping verbs.
How **was** the exam? Not easy.
Were you there when the accident happened? Yes, I was./No, I wasn't.

The Past Progressive Tense: *Stop the Video and Replay that Scene!*

Use past progressive to report an ongoing past action or condition in the past, when you don't know the time it began or ended. Imagine that a friend asks you about a movie he/she hasn't seen. You need to explain the opening setting of the movie as well as the main actions and characters. The past progressive is like this opening setting; that is, it serves as a background against which the major actions occur. For example: *This movie was set in World War II. At the beginning, soldiers were climbing up a hill and singing a song to themselves. They were walking as if they were tired. Suddenly, a huge blast came out of the sky, and the soldiers all dove to the ground.*

The past progressive tense is used with either a specific time in the past or another past tense verb (simple or progressive).

1. **To tell what someone was doing at a specific time in the past:**
   At nine o'clock last night, Maria **was sitting** on the couch.
   In September 2002, I **was working** in Siberia.

2. **In questions of interrogation (especially on TV police shows when the detective interviews the criminal):**
   What **were** you **wearing** last Saturday night?
   What **were** you **doing** on the night of July 6?

Forming the Past Progressive Tense

Statements and Questions

To form the past progressive tense, use the past form of *be* + the present participle (*-ing* form) of the verb.
I **was talking** to my parents when my roommate came in.
At 6:00, we **were waiting** for a table in the restaurant.
He **wasn't studying** at the library last Wednesday night.
Were they **drinking** wine while they **were cooking**?
Where **were** they **going** last night?

Time Indicators

The past progressive tense is often used in time clauses with *while, as,* and *just as.*

1. If the two subjects are the same or if the information in the second clause refers to the subject in the first clause, the main clause generally uses simple past.

   While Hilda **was living** in Colombia, she *worked* at a veterinary hospital.
   While I **was sleeping** last night, the phone *rang* and *woke* me up.

2. If the two subjects are different and the actions are taking place in different locations, two past progressive verbs may be used.

   As I **was arguing** with my brother in the living room, my sister and mother **were chatting** happily in the kitchen.
   Just as Bill **was walking** into his apartment, a thief **was escaping** through the window.

3. When the adverb *when* is used with the simple past tense (to note a past event), the past progressive tense is sometimes used in the other clause.

   When I met John, I **was living** in Philadelphia.
   I **was driving** to work when I heard about the robbery.

Comma Use with Time Clauses

Use a comma after the time clause if it comes before the main clause in a sentence.

While you were talking to your professor, Jen was standing behind you.

Just as they walked in the door, the phone rang.

If a time clause comes after the main clause, no comma is needed.

Jen was standing behind you while you were talking to your professor.

The phone rang just as they walked in the door.

■ 2-1 Punctuation

Read the sentences below. Each sentence contains a time indicator. Some need commas, and some do not. If a sentence needs a comma, insert it in the appropriate place.

Example: When I went to sleep, they were still talking.

1. Last weekend Marco went to the movies.

2. While we were watching the game she ordered a pizza.

3. As soon as they saw their grades Anna and Luke called their parents to celebrate.

4. The bookstore was very crowded when I arrived.

5. Peter didn't realize his book was gone until he got to class.

6. In September 2003 I was traveling around Thailand.

■ 2-2 Sentence Writing

Read each topic below. Decide if you should use simple past or past progressive for each topic; then, write appropriate sentences.

A. Write three sentences about what you did on your last vacation.

Example: Last year, I went to San Diego. I visited the zoo and walked on the beach.

1. _____

2. _____

3. _____

B. Write three sentences about what happened in the news in the last few days.

Example: Yesterday, there was a car accident. A driver ran into a large bus on a busy street.

4. _____

5. _____

6. _____

C. Write four sentences about what you were doing in 2005. Where were you living? Where were you working?

Example: In 2005, I was living on campus in a dorm. I was working in the chemistry lab.

7. _____

8. _____

9. _____

10. _____

D. Write four sentences to describe the weather last week.

Example: Early last week, it was warm and sunny. Then, it rained for two days. Finally, it stopped raining.

11. _____

12. _____

13. _____

14. _____

E. Write four sentences about what you liked or disliked about high school.

Example: I met some great people in high school. I had a lot of fun learning languages. I didn't like math.

15. _____

16. _____

17. _____

18. _____

F. There was a robbery at the mall last night at seven. Write four sentences telling (the police) where you were and what you were doing at that time.

Example: At 7:00, I was in the mall. I was eating ice cream at the food court. My friend and I were waiting for her sister to pick us up. We weren't standing near the door.

19. _____

20. _____

21. _____

22. _____

■ 2-3 Description of the Illustration

Look at the picture below. Use it to complete the activities.

A. Imagine that you are an archeologist (someone who studies past civilizations) in the year 2239. You have found the object in the picture. Write a paragraph telling what you think the object is. Tell when, where, and why it was made. Tell who made it and how it was used. Use the simple past tense.

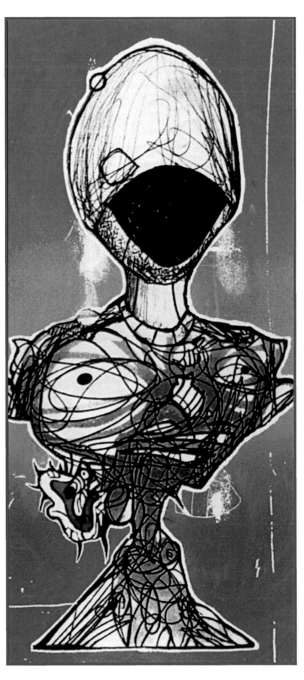

B. Think about your life when you were a child vs. your life today. Where did you live? What did you do for fun? What kinds of things do you have now that you didn't have then? What would children today think about your childhood? Write the answers in your notebook.

■ 2-4 Communicative Activity

With a partner, read the actions in Sequence A. Talk about each action and decide what order they occurred in. Number the actions so that they follow a logical sequence. The first action is numbered "1" for you. When you and your partner finish Sequence A, discuss and number the actions in Sequence B.

Sequence A

____ We eventually decided to just stay home and enjoy the fire.

____ We decided that we wanted to be alone.

____ We made some coffee.

____ We thought about making a fire and staying home.

____ We discussed going to a movie.

____ We saw that the weather would be cold and rainy.

_1_ We woke up unusually early that day.

____ We looked through the newspaper to find the movie section.

____ We sat down to drink the coffee and decide how to spend the day.

____ We saw an advertisement for an auction that day.

____ We planned to call our friends to join us.

____ We ate some bagels with cream cheese.

Sequence B

____ Anatoly wanted to take the train.

____ They looked at hundreds of paintings.

____ Anatoly looked forward to seeing the Byzantine exhibition.

____ They decided to have lunch.

____ They often visited the Moscow art museums.

____ They planned to go to the Metropolitan Museum of Art on Fifth Avenue.

____ They ate at the Museum coffee shop.

____ Ludmilla wanted to drive into the city.

_1_ Anatoly and Ludmilla decided to go to New York City for the day.

____ They lived most of their lives in Russia.

____ Ludmilla looked forward to seeing the Impressionists.

____ They thought about strolling through the streets of Moscow.

____ They discussed the paintings they had seen.

____ They got very tired.

____ They walked for over a mile through the museum.

____ They had a great day.

Read each topic below. Make sure you understand the questions. Work in groups of four to discuss the first topic. Then choose one person to report the group's answers to the class. Next, move to another group to discuss the next topic. Repeat this process until all the topics are discussed.

A. "Forget about yesterday. It's over and done with." Has anyone ever said that to you? That may be good advice but not always so easy to follow. Discuss certain times in your life that you still cannot forget about. Explain why those times and actions still have an effect on your life.

B. Marcel Proust wrote about the power of the past in *Remembrance of Things Past.* In this work, he said that the sense that most powerfully brought the past back was the sense of smell. When you go back into your memory, do you associate people, places, or things with smell? When you smell bread baking, do you think of your mother or grandmother? When you smell a fire burning, what memory comes to mind? Describe what certain smells make you think about.

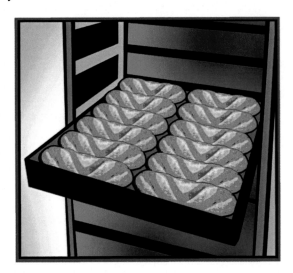

C. Did you have a part in history? Were you in a place where something happened that later appeared in history books? Did you know someone who had an influence over history, even a small part of history? Discuss how you are a part of the history of your culture and family. Everyone is a part of history, even if they are not in the history books.

D. An English student lost a ruby ring that her father had made for her because the ruby was her birthstone. After her father died, she couldn't stop thinking about this lost ring. Did you ever lose something that was important to you? Discuss something you lost and the memories and stories associated with it.

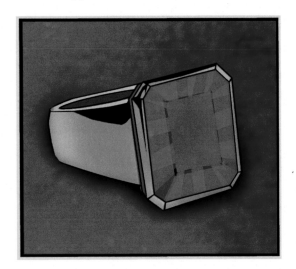

■ 2-6 Grammar Practice

Make each verb phrase into a time clause. Then, combine it with the second clause to make a complete sentence. Remember that by using *when* with two short actions, you will create a sequence of actions. When you use *while*, you will create a long background action and a short action, or two long background actions that occur at the same time.

Examples:

> When I sliced the bread, I made a sandwich.
> When I made the sandwich, I also sliced the bread.
> While I was slicing the bread, my husband was making a sandwich.
> While I was making a sandwich, he was slicing the bread.

1. move my chair/bend my knee _____

_____

_____

2. movie start/stop talking _____

_____

_____

3. eat hamburger/wish it were salmon _____

_____

4. research lives of presidents/discover information about the assassination of McKinley _____

_____

_____

5. talk to mother on phone/sob uncontrollably _____

_____

_____

6. try on a size 8 dress/realize it doesn't fit _____

_____

_____

7. adjust to rejection by my friends/be sad _____

_____

_____

■ 2-7 Description of the Photograph

Imagine you are at the archeological site in the picture below. Use it to complete the activites with a partner.

Cave Dwellings Discovered by Dr. Herrera and the University of Bogotá Team

A. Last month, Dr. Luisa Herrera and her team from the University of Bogotá, Colombia, discovered a series of cave dwellings. Dr. Herrera wants to hear your thoughts about the people who lived in these caves. Use the picture to answer the questions below.

   1. Who do you think lived in the caves?

   _____

   _____

   _____

   2. What did these people eat? How did they survive?

   _____

   _____

   _____

B. Now compare your answers with a partner's. Then work with your partner to write a story in your notebook about the people who lived in the caves. Include information about the people who lived there, what they did, what they ate, and how they survived.

■ 2-8 Error Correction

Read the sentences below. Each sentence has at least one mistake. The mistakes could be in subject–verb agreement, simple past vs. past progressive, or missing words. Underline all the mistakes in each sentence. Then write the sentence correctly. Review the list of irregular past verbs in the Appendix if needed.

1. While Sam <u>driving</u> to school, he <u>was seeing</u> an accident.

   While Sam was driving to school, he saw an accident.

2. Last month, Professor Jacobson finded a wallet in the student center.

   _____

   _____

3. When Marta finishes the book last night, she takes a break.

   _____

   _____

4. Helga born in 1981. She spended her youth in a small town where her mother teached.

   _____

   _____

5. Nancy Rosen keeped her name after she get married last year.

   _____

   _____

6. Horace quitted his job when he founded out that everyone gets a raise but him.

   _____

   _____

7. Someone stealed the bag that Yeng Yu hided under the table.

   _____

   _____

8. The students writed paragraphs while the professor correcting the their grammar tests.

   _____

   _____

Read the passage below. Highlight or underline all the verbs you find. When you finish, discuss the passage with a partner. What tenses were used? Why?

My Worst Professor

I will never forget Professor Schlessingham, who taught Medieval Literature at a university in New York City. I should not say that he was egotistical, uncreative, antisocial, uncaring, and boring, that he didn't care about students. But I will tell a story to illustrate my point.

It was a snowy Monday morning in February. The snow started at 6:00 the night before, and by 11:00 a.m. the next day, there were more than two feet on the ground. Since the school was in New York and most people either walked or took the subway, it never closed for snow. Professor Schlessingham lived in Connecticut, 75 miles away. There was no way that he was coming.

I lived in a dormitory on campus, and the classroom building was twenty yards away. I left my nice, warm room and walked into the storm. I couldn't see three feet ahead because of the wind and snow. The class started at 11:30. When I walked into the classroom, I turned on the lights and sat in the middle of the room. I never expected to see anyone that day.

I took out my book. It was *Beowulf*, an old English poem. When I heard the weather forecast the day before, I didn't read the book. At 11:35, I looked out the window. It was still snowing hard. Just at that moment, the door opened, and a snowman came in. He walked in, took off his coat and hat, and took his position in front of the room. It was Professor Schlessingham. I couldn't believe it. He took out his old yellow notes and started to read in his dry monotone. Every five minutes or so, he looked up and asked, "Any questions?" Since I had no idea what the book was about, I stayed quiet. This continued for almost an hour. Finally, he put away his notes, walked to the corner of the room, put on his coat and hat, and left. He didn't look at me or say a word to me—about the weather or about the fact that I was the only student in the class.

The next Wednesday, the class was filled with students. Professor Schlessingham walked into the room, took out the old yellow notes and said, "Let's continue our discussion of *Beowulf*." One of the students raised his hand. "Professor, what do you mean, 'continue'? We didn't even start talking about *Beowulf*. We were supposed to start on Monday, but that was the day of the snowstorm." Professor Schlessingham said, "We had class Monday." All the students replied, "Are you kidding? It snowed three feet! How many students came?" Professor Schlessingham said, "I don't know. We discussed the beginning and middle of the poem. Get notes from the students who were here!" Everyone looked around the room and asked "Were you here?" "Who was stupid enough to come out in the snow for a class?"

I said, "I was the only one here, but I didn't take any notes." "What an idiot," they all yelled at me. So instead of getting credit for coming to class, I only made my fellow students angry at me.

"Too bad for all of you," said Professor Schlessingham. We never talked about the beginning or middle of *Beowulf*, and we even had a test the next class about the parts everyone missed. Needless to say, everyone failed the test, including me, which made Professor Schlessingham extremely happy.

The story below is about a strange day on a college campus. Read the story and write a verb from the list below in each blank in the simple past tense. You will use some verbs more than once. Remember to make the verbs and subjects agree.

arrive	be	begin	come	decide
discuss	drive	get	have	hear
leave	lie	meet	plan	prepare
ring	say	scream	shiver	spin
stop	wait	want	wake	wonder

Alarm

Last month, it snowed for three days. Then, the temperature dropped, and there **(1)** _____was_____

a sheet of solid ice on the ground and the roads. On the second day, I **(2)** _____ to

work on Lincoln Avenue when my car **(3)** _____ out of control and **(4)** _____

to circle around. I **(5)** _____ . Finally, I **(6)** _____ control of the car again.

After I **(7)** _____ at college, I **(8)** _____ that classes **(9)** _____

that day, so I **(10)** _____ my notes for class. While I **(11)** _____ my class, four

students from the class **(12)** _____ to my office and **(13)** _____ that they

(14) _____ to go home because of the weather.

While we **(15)** _____ whether we should stay or go home, an alarm bell

(16) _____ , so we all **(17)** _____ the building and **(18)** _____ for

the alarm to stop ringing. We **(19)** _____ the whole time we **(20)** _____ for the

bell to stop. Finally, the bell **(21)** _____ , and we **(22)** _____ to go home.

Later that week, several students were absent. Then, I **(23)** _____ one day that week

with a very sore throat. It turns out that all of us **(24)** _____ the flu for two weeks.

While we **(25)** _____ in bed with the flu, we **(26)** _____ why the college was

open on that fateful day of the ringing alarm bell.

2-11 Sentence Stems

Read the sentence stems below. Write statements about yourself using simple past or past progressive tense in either a main clause or a time clause.

1. When I lived in my native country, *I worked very hard every day.* _____

   _____

2. After I got a cell phone, _____

   _____

3. Before I got married, _____

   _____

4. While I was walking to the library, _____

   _____

5. I did not have a car _____

   _____

6. They wanted to see the exhibit _____

   _____

7. I hoped to see him _____

   _____

8. I brushed my teeth after _____

   _____

9. While I was jogging last night, _____

   _____

10. As I was getting up this morning, _____

   _____

11. I was studying last week when _____

   _____

The Past Tense: Simple and Progressive

■ 2-12 Description of the Photograph

Look at the photograph below. Use it to complete the activities.

A. In your notebook, write a paragraph that describes the relationship shown between the siblings (brother and sister) in the photograph. Since this photograph was taken a long time ago, use the simple past or past progressive tense in your paragraph.

B. In your notebook, write a paragraph about your childhood. Use simple past and past progressive. When you were young, what was your relationship with your siblings? Who were you closest to? If you are an only child, write about whether you wanted a brother or sister or if you were happy to be the one and only.

■ 2-13 Unit Review

Directed Writing

Task: Write a three-paragraph essay describing a special day in your life.

Prewriting

Think of a special day in your life. For example, it could be a birthday or wedding, the day you started your first job, the day you met a special person, or the day you arrived in the United States. In your notebook, write down as many details as you can remember about where you were, who was with you, and what happened that day. Use idea maps like the ones below. If you were very young and need more details, ask any friends and family who were there to tell you what they remember.

My Special Day: _____

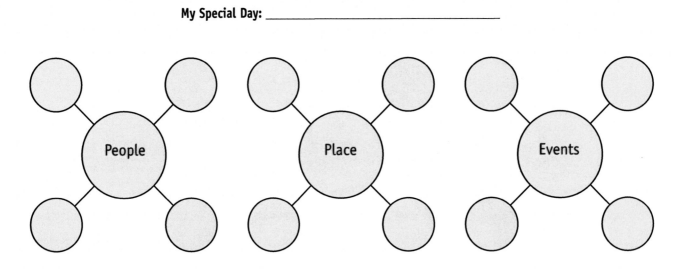

First Draft

Write a first draft of your essay. Use your idea maps and notes to organize your ideas as you write. Check that the first sentence of each paragraph states the main idea of the paragraph. Use simple past verbs to report actions or conditions that were completed; use past progressive verbs to describe the setting of the event. Don't forget to indent the first line and write the main idea sentence at the beginning of each paragraph. Include as much information as you can about your special day, including why it was so special to you.

> **Model** One special day in my life was my 18th birthday. It was special because I was finally an adult. There were so many things I wanted to do . . .
>
> The first thing I wanted to do was buy my own car. When I woke up that morning, I bugged my dad to take me to the car dealership . . .
>
> The best thing about my birthday was the party in the evening . . .

Revision

Read through your essay and check for use of simple past, past progressive, time indicators, clear main idea and details, and correct spelling and punctuation, Pay particular attention to the use of commas after time clauses. Share your essay with a partner. Your partner should be able to answer the following questions about your essay:

- What was your special day? Why was it so special?
- Where did the event take place? Who was there, and what happened that day?
- Did you use the correct simple past and past progressive forms in the correct manner?
- Do you have any errors in spelling or punctuation?
- Does the essay need any more information?

Final Draft

Make any changes or additions that are needed in your essay. Then write or type a final copy. You may want to include your final essay in a portfolio of your writing.

Evaluation

Your teacher will grade your essay. You will be evaluated on:

- clarity of main ideas and level of supporting detail in your essay;
- correct use and forms for simple past and past progressive; and
- appropriate use of time indicators, including correct punctuation.

Unit 3

The Future Tense

This unit will address some of the forms, meanings, and uses you need to know in order to talk and write about the future. The future tense is used in the following situations:

1. **to express thought**

   We usually approach our future plans by thinking about them. Future forms that imply thought include:

   A. *be going to* + base verb for definite plans that are close to the present

   After class, I **am going to take** a nap.

   After she finishes the report, Barbara **is going to bring** it to the office.

   B. *will* + base verb for more formal/distant plans or immediate decisions

   One day, Mary **will be** a published author.

   I guess **I'll take** the brown purse.

   C. *plan to* + base verb for strategies that were thought about

   I **plan to get** my degree in art.

   Dr. Johnson **plans to retire** at the end of the year.

   D. *intend to* + base verb for definite plans that require determination

   No matter what, I **intend to see** her today.

   We **intend to find** jobs before graduation.

Some aspects of the future can be addressed with fixed expressions. These expressions are the same every time they are used.

   It is important that + *I, he, she,* etc. + base verb to stress importance

   It is (really) important that you call me tonight.

   It is important that he be on time for the examination tomorrow.

   It is critical that + *I, he, she,* etc. + base verb to stress urgency

   It is critical that the patient gets blood now.

   It is critical that they arrive in New York by 3:00.

2. **to express emotions**

   Sometimes we consider the future with emotion.

   A. *want to* + base verb to express longing

   She **wants to marry** him.

   We really **want to buy** a house this year.

   B. *hope to* + base verb to express a wish or expectation

   I **hope to get** a letter from home today.

   My mother **hopes to finish** all the invitations by tonight.

   C. *want/hope* + *to be able to* + base verb to express a desire for ability

   I **want to be able to understand** at least some Italian when I go to Italy next year.

   I **hope to be able to attend** the party. I'll try my best.

   D. *hope* + *that* + clause for a hope expressed in a clause

   I **hope that Smitty will win the election.**

   I **hope that the happy couple is still happy one year from now.**

The Future Progressive Tense

The future progressive tense is used to imagine or plan what will be going on at a later time.

> By the time I'm forty, I **will be living** in Michigan far away from my parents.
> Tonight, **he's going to be making** ice cream, so don't bother him.
> Next Monday, **we'll be skiing** in Colorado.

Forming the Future Progressive Tense

To form the future progressive tense, use *will be* or *be going to be* + the *-ing* form.

Affirmative and Negative Statements

Next week, **I'm going to be running** a lot of errands.
This afternoon, Tanya **will be driving** home.
They're going to be attending classes in Korea this January.
When you're older, you **won't be lying** on the beach in Bermuda.
Jun **isn't going to be graduating** next spring.
We **won't be bringing** drinks to the picnic tomorrow.

Yes/No and Information Questions and Short Answers

Will I **be attending** class on Monday?	**Yes, I will. / No,** I **won't.**
Will Shana **be singing** at the concert Thursday?	**Yes,** she **will. / No,** she **won't.**
Are we **going to be reading** novels this semester?	**Yes, we are. / No,** we **aren't.**
How much **will** you **be spending** on vacation?	I don't know.
Where **is** he **going to be living** next year?	In his own apartment.
When **will** they **be moving**?	March.

Talking About Another Time or Condition: What Ifs

We can also consider the future starting from another time or in another condition.

1. *if* + present tense + future tense clause for actions that depend on certain conditions.
   If I **get** into Harvard, I **will go** there.
   If he really **loves** her, he **will move** to Antarctica with her.
   They **will visit** their grandmother **if** they **have** time tomorrow.

2. *wish* + *that* + clause to express a wish that might not come true
   I **wish** (that) you **would drive** me to school.
   I **wish** (that) you **could come** over tonight.
   They **wish** (that) you **were going to be** at their wedding.
   Note: In these cases, *that* may be omitted.

Future Tense with Time Clauses

In time clauses beginning with *when, after, before, as soon as, once,* and *until* for actions that will happen at the same time as other future actions, the sequence of tenses is very important.

Subject + Verb (simple future), Time Word + Subject + Verb (simple present)
I **will work** hard **until** the job **is** done.
She'**ll finish** the project **before** she **leaves** for the weekend.
We **will have** a big party **as soon as** he **comes** back from the Air Force.

or

Time Word + Subject + Verb (simple present), Subject + Verb (simple future)
Once James **pays** his credit card bill, he **will start** to save some money.
Until I **get** a reliable car, I **won't take** any long road trips.
When my parents **visit**, I **will show** them all the sights.

Note: When a time clause appears at the beginning of a sentence, separate it from the main clause with a comma.

■ 3-1 Punctuation

Read the groups of words below. Arrange them to make a correct English sentence and write it on the line. Insert a comma in the correct place if one is needed. When you are finished, practice reading the full sentence aloud with a partner. Be careful to pause if you see a comma.

1. as soon as promoted David get raise he is will a big

   David will get a big raise as soon as he is promoted. OR. As soon as he is promoted, David will get a big raise.

2. are on when Mike and going our parents we I are vacation to visit

   _____

3. gets will Li school if he quit the job not

   _____

4. to study need until improve you will every day your grades

   _____

5. going if Gonzalo and go it is to Mark to class won't snow

   _____

6. a lot of spend shopping when go we money will probably Jen and I

   _____

7. research start will before my I several topics I paper

   _____

8. home everyone Helen after comes work make from dinner will for she

   _____

■ 3-2 Sentence Writing

For each structure below, write a sentence about yourself or your family. Compare your sentences with the examples in the Unit Introduction and make any necessary corrections. Share your sentences with the class.

1. *hope to* + base verb _____

2. *plan to* + base verb _____

3. wish + that clause _____

4. *want to* + base verb _____

5. *be going to be* + *-ing* form _____

6. *It is important that* + subject + base verb _____

7. *intend to* + base verb _____

8. *will* _____

9. *It is critical that* + subject + base verb _____

10. *want/hope* + *to be able to* + base verb _____

11. *hope* + *that* clause _____

12. *if/whether* + present tense + future tense clause _____

_____

13. *After* + present tense + future tense clause _____

_____

14. *As soon as* + present tense + future tense clause _____

_____

15. *Until* + present tense + future tense clause _____

_____

16. *By the end of this month* + future progressive _____

_____

Look at the photograph below. Use it to complete the activities.

A. This photo was taken in Sri Lanka. In your notebook, write a paragraph describing the photograph. Use the present tense to describe what you see. Answer these questions: Where are the children? What are they doing? Who is the person in the background?

B. Now imagine the future of the two young people you see. In your notebook, write a paragraph telling about their future lives. Answer these questions: What will they be doing in 10 years? Will they have an education? Are they going to be staying in Sri Lanka or traveling to other countries?

■ 3-4 Communicative Activity

Paired Writing

Each story below has a beginning and an ending. You and your partner have to write the middle section. Use the phrases and clauses provided for each story to write sentences that lead logically from the story beginning to the end. Make sure your new sentences use the appropriate tense.

Story 1

plan to + base verb	*Once he/she knows*	*hope that* + clause
It is critical that + clause	*want to be able to*	*wish that he/she would*

Lorelei stared at the back of the man 10 feet in front of her at the crowded exhibition of Egyptian
treasures at the Field Museum of Natural History. After all these years, could that man be Sam?

_____

_____

_____

_____

_____

Then she said to herself, "If I don't tap
him on the shoulder now, I will never know whether my true love has eluded me once more."

Story 2

is/are going to	*plan to* + base verb	*Until he hears from them*
wish(es) that they could	*intend to* + base verb	*If he sues them*
He has decided that he will		

Jack doesn't know whether to look for a new job or to apply to the firm he worked for last summer.

_____

_____

_____

_____

Finally, he decided to let bygones be bygones, forget the past, and move on.

Read each topic below. Make sure you understand the questions. Work in groups of four to discuss the first topic. Choose one person to report the group's answers to the class. Then move to another group to discuss the next topic. Repeat this process until all the topics are discussed.

A. There are many expressions that express attitudes towards the future. "What will be, will be" is one. "Move on" is another. Do you know what these expressions mean? Discuss these and other English sayings or idioms that convey attitudes towards the future. Also, discuss sayings and idioms in your native language that deal with the future. What do these attitudes reveal about people's comfort with the future?

B. Have you ever had an accident or illness that caused you to think about death? Or has the death of someone close to you caused you to think about the end of time? Did this thinking change your attitude toward your future? If so, in what specific ways?

C. What are some things that you swore (promised) you would never do, but you did? What are some things that you now swear you will never do? Discuss some future situations that might make your current "nevers" into "maybes."

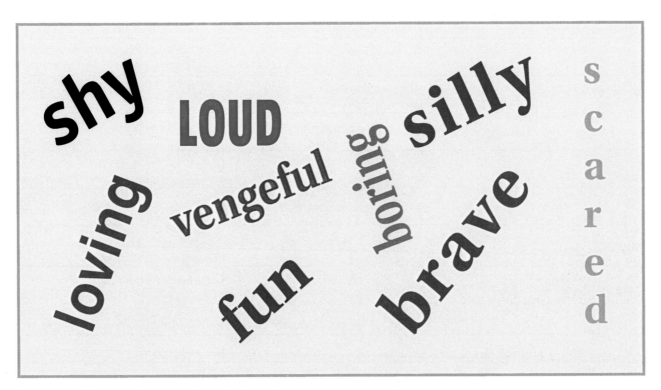

D. It has been said that the past predicts the future. In your notebook, write down one or two of your most obvious character traits. Think about what people have said about you in the past. Were you described as loving, vengeful, shy, loud, fun, boring, silly, brave, scared? Once you have identified one or two of your outstanding characteristics, predict how those characteristics will affect your future.

■ 3-6 Grammar in Action

Planning Your Future

A. The future is a tunnel of mystery. There is so much that is out of our control. Yet despite the uncertainty, people look to the future and make specific plans. Make a list of eight things you hope to achieve in life.

Future Achievements

1. _____

   _____

2. _____

   _____

3. _____

   _____

   _____

4. _____

   _____

5. _____

   _____

   _____

6. _____

   _____

7. _____

   _____

8. _____

   _____

B. Use your list from Exercise A and the future tense expressions from the Unit Introduction to write a paragraph in your notebook about your plans for the future. Where do you see yourself in 10 years? What job will you have? Will you have a family? Where will you live? When you are finished, share your paragraph with a partner. Does your partner think you will reach your goals? Why or why not?

■ 3-7 Communicative Activity

Work in groups of three or four. Read each situation below. Think of two possible actions that could follow the particular circumstances. Use any future tense expression to explain what happens next.

Example: Chad's girlfriend has just told him that she doesn't want to see him anymore. What will he do next?

a. _He will cry all night._

b. _He will immediately call her best friend, Cindy, who has been in love with him for a month._

1. Sid lost $2000, his mortgage payment, at the racetrack. What will he do next?

   a. _____

   b. _____

2. Mr. Peter Janiak, 59 years old with two grown children, has just been fired from his job. What will he do?

   a. _____

   b. _____

3. Henrietta has been offered a job, but she has to move to California. What will she do?

   a. _____

   b. _____

4. Cho finds a wallet on the floor of the cafeteria. She has no money, but she is an honest person. What will she do?

   a. _____

   b. _____

5. Manav Patel's mother-in-law has just called. She is coming to visit for four months. What will Manav do next?

   a. _____

   b. _____

6. Christine, a 17-year-old driver, was caught speeding on the highway. She has to go to court. She was driving 101 in a 55-mph zone. What will happen in court?

   a. _____

   b. _____

7. Cornelius gets a call from his friend, Joe. Joe has an extra ticket for the big L.A. Lakers–Miami Heat game. However, Cornelius promised to take his girlfriend out the same night because it is their six-month anniversary. What will Cornelius do?

   a. _____

   b. _____

Imagining Your Dream House

Many people in the United States hope to own a home someday. They have a "dream house" in their mind. It is a special place that has exactly what they want: the ideal location (in the mountains, on a lake, on the main street of a city), the right number of rooms, the perfect style. On the lines below, write a paragraph about your dream house. Use as many of the future expressions from the Unit Introduction as you can. Answer these questions: Where is your dream home? What is the view from your house? What style is your dream house? Is it a cottage, like the one in the illustration, or a mansion? What will it look like outside? How many rooms do you want? What will the rooms be like? How long will it take you to get your dream home?

_____

_____

_____

_____

_____

_____

■ 3-9 Error Correction

There are mistakes in the story below. The mistakes could be in subject-verb agreement, present vs. future, or missing words. With a partner, underline all the mistakes you find. Rewrite the story and correct the mistakes.

Eddie Thinks About Choosing a Pet

For as long as he can remember, Eddie has wanted a pet. Now that he is 10, his parents have finally said that he can have one. Now he has to think about what kind of pet to get. His mother has said that it be critical that his pet is easy to train. She doesn't care whether he will get a dog, a puppy, a cat, a kitten, a guinea pig, a rabbit, or even a ferret, but the pet must be trainable or kept in a cage. His mother doesn't plan clean up after a messy pet. Eddie hopes be able going to an animal shelter the coming weekend. He want to see all of the animals that are available for adoption before he will make up his mind. Once he will see the adult and the baby animals, he knows whether he will want a baby that he intends will train himself, or an adult that he won't have to train. It is important that he holds the animals one by one. He planning to spending a lot of time at the animal shelter so that he will be able to observe the "souls" of the animals. He has decided that whichever pet he chooses, the pet connects with his own soul.

_____

_____

_____

_____

_____

_____

_____

_____

_____

_____

_____

_____

■ 3-10 Grammar Practice

Unscrambling Sentences

Work with a partner. Unscramble the words below to make a clear and correct sentence about the future. Use all the words. Write the correct sentence on the lines.

1. on be a Harriet to to finish hopes career note high able her

   Harriet hopes to be able to finish her career on a high note.
   _____

2. have soda I will a

   _____

   _____

3. understand that it my is you problems important

   _____

   _____

4. dinner if paid tonight today will to we out he go gets

   _____

   _____

5. June to my are neighbors in move going

   _____

   _____

6. be account daughter I to able create for want an my to

   _____

   _____

7. next married be Aaron Renee will getting month and

   _____

   _____

8. mail plan to their tomorrow I gift California wedding to

   _____

   _____

■ 3-11 Sentence Stems

Use the sentence stems below to write statements about the future. Write both affirmative and negative statements. Make sure the subjects and verbs agree and that you choose the appropriate tense.

1. If you really need my assistance, _I will be happy to help._ _____

2. When the fire alarm rings, _____

3. After I finish this paper, _____

4. At precisely 9:00 p.m. tomorrow, _____

5. Unless you say you're sorry, _____

6. Next winter, _____

7. In five years, _____

8. Three years from now, Helga _____

9. If I win the lottery, _____

10. When your father gets home, _____

■ 3-12 Sentence Conclusions

Use the sentence conclusions below to write statements about the future. Write both affirmative and negative statements. Make sure the subjects and verbs agree and that you choose the appropriate tense.

1. _____ _I never want to see him_ _____ again as long as I live.

2. _____ I will come running to help you.

3. _____ before Mom comes home.

4. _____ when he gets home.

5. _____ after he cleans up all the empty beer bottles.

6. _____ tomorrow at nine.

7. _____ until my girlfriend gets back from her business trip.

8. _____ unless he apologizes.

9. _____ after Bob graduates.

10. _____ when Sidney finally wakes up.

■ 3-13 Communicative Activity

Interview a classmate. Write a paragraph. Make an oral presentation.

Use questions like the samples below to interview three classmates about their future plans. Take notes in the chart. In your notebook, write a short paragraph about each classmate. When you are finished, choose one of your paragraphs to share with the class.

Sample questions:

What *is* your name and where *are* you from?

What *are* you *going to do* after you *finish* the English program?

Do you *plan to return* to your country from time to time? How often?

Do you *intend to continue studying* at this college or another college?

What *will* you *study*? (*What will* your major *be*?)

What kind of job *will* you *have* in five years?

Are you *going to* stay in the U.S.?

What city *do* you *hope to live* in?

Classmate 1	Classmate 2	Classmate 3

Directed Writing

Task: Write a three-paragraph essay about a goal you hope to achieve in the future.

Prewriting

We all have dreams about the future, some of which can turn into achievable goals. It may be to discover a cure for a cancer, write a great novel, become a well-known politician, sing in a concert, marry a childhood sweetheart, or even star in a movie. Think of a life goal you would like to achieve. What will you do to learn what you have to know in order to achieve your goal? How would you define it? What will your first steps be? What will you be doing when you have achieved your goal? In your notebook, make notes about the goal. Use a chart like the one below.

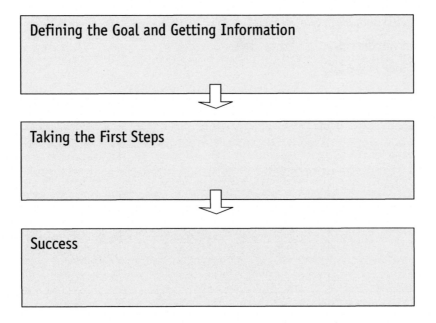

Defining the Goal and Getting Information

Taking the First Steps

Success

First Draft

Write a first draft of your essay. Use your chart and notes to organize your ideas as you write. Check that your first paragraph defines your goal and explains how you will be doing to get the information you need to know in order to achieve it. Make sure that your third paragraph shows how you will know when you have achieved your goal. Use future tense verbs to express thoughts and emotions; use future progressive verbs to imagine and plan. Remember to indent the first line in each paragraph of your essay.

> **Model** I have always dreamed about walking on the moon, a goal I will pursue with diligence. To achieve this goal, I will find out all I can about NASA. I will also find out the courses I need to take in order...
>
> For the next five years I will be preparing for a career in engineering. I will build on the math and science courses, by taking...
>
> I will also be trying to meet...
>
> In 2010, I will achieve my goal. I will be working in Houston at NASA as a...
>
> I will be...

Revision

Read through your essay and check for correct usage of the future and future progressive tenses, time clauses, clear main idea and details, and correct spelling and punctuation. Share your essay with a partner. Your partner should be able to answer the following questions about your essay:

- What is the goal?
- How will you achieve the goal?
- What will be doing to prove you have achieved the goal?
- How will life be better in the future?
- Did you use correct forms of the future and future progressive tenses?
- Did you use correct sequence of tenses in sentences with time clauses?
- Do you have any errors in spelling or punctuation?
- Does the essay need any more information?

Final Draft

Make any changes or additions that are needed in your essay. Then write or type a final copy. You may want to include your final essay in a portfolio of your writing.

Evaluation

Your teacher will grade your essay. You will be evaluated on:

- clarity of ideas and level of supporting detail in your essay;
- correct use and forms of for future and future progressive; and
- appropriate time clauses with the future.

Unit 4

Questions

One of the most difficult grammar tasks in English is forming questions. The typical subject–verb word order is often inverted. Tenses sometimes change, and modals or the auxiliary verbs *be*, *have*, or *do* are inserted into the sentence. *Have* is used to form the perfect tenses, which you will learn in units 5 and 6. You will study modals further in units 7 and 8. Study the box below to learn key auxiliaries for forming questions in English.

Forming Questions

When forming questions in English, we add an auxiliary verb to the base form. The auxiliary verb is the one that matches subject and tense. For each type of question, there is a specific word order.

Key Auxiliary Verbs for English Questions

Do	Be	Modals	
Do	Am	Can	Could
Does	Is	Will	Would
Did	Are	Shall	Should
	Was	May	
	Were		

Yes/No Questions

For questions whose answers are *Yes* or *No* (*Yes/No* questions), the word order is: X—S—V (Auxiliary—Subject—Verb)

Yes/No Questions with Be

The word order for *Yes/No* questions with *be* is V—S (*Be*—Subject). In *Yes/No* questions with *be*, change the auxiliary form to match the subject: *am, is, are* for present tense and *was* or *were* for past tense. Add the *-ing* form of the main verb for present or past progressive questions. Use *am, is,* or *are* + *going to* + base verb for future tense.

Present

Am I in the right room?
V   S   (prepositional phrase)

Are you angry with me?
V   S   (adjective) (prepositional phrase)

Is Carlos **flying** here from Brazil?
V   S   V   (prepositional phrase)

Are they **joining** us for dinner?
V   S   V   (object) (prepositional phrase)

Past

Was I wrong?
V   S   (adjective)

Were you **waiting** for us?
V   S   V   (object)

Was the dishwasher **running** at 9:00?
V   S   V

Were the phones **ringing** tonight?
V   S   V

Future

Are you **going to study** engineering next year?
V   S   V   (object)

Is the cake **going to taste** OK?
V   S   V   (adjective)

The word order X—S—V (Auxiliary—Subject—Verb) is the same for all subjects and tenses.

Questions with *Do*

For present tense questions, use *Do* for all subjects except *he, she,* and *it*. For those three subjects, use *Does*.

Do I **like** popcorn?
X S V (object)

Do you **buy** your books online?
X S V   (object)

Does Han **speak** Chinese?
X S V (object)

Do they **want** to come with us?
X S V

For past tense *Yes/No* questions, use *Did* the for all subjects.

Did Karen **go** to school last year?
X S V (object)

Did they **read** the article before class?
X S V (object)

In questions with modals, use the same modal for all subjects.

May I **eat** another cookie?
X S V   (object)

Can you **take** notes for me in psychology?
X S V   (object)

Should Viktor **work** for his father?
X S V

Will we **finish** the project on time?
X S V   (object)

Information Questions

For questions whose answers are specific information, the word order is:

Q—X—S—V (Question word—Auxiliary—Subject—Verb).

The English question words are *Who, What, When, Where, Why, Whose, How, How much* and *How many*.

Information Questions with *Be*

The word order for information questions with *be* is Q—V—S (Question word—Verb—Subject) In information questions with *be*, change the auxiliary to match the subject: *am, is, are* for present tense and *was* or *were* for past tense. Add the *-ing* to the main verb form for present or past progressive questions. Use *am, is,* or *are* + *going to* + base verb for future tense.

Where is your friend?
Q V S

Who are you **going to go out** with on Saturday?
Q V S   V   (prepositional phrase)

Why was she **leaving?**
Q V S V

How are we **going to get** to class next week?
Q V S V   (prepositional phrase)

Information Questions with *do* and *did*

For present tense questions, use the auxiliary *do* for all subjects except *he, she,* and *it*. For those subjects, use *does*. For past tense questions, use the auxiliary *did* for all subjects.

When do I **get** my grades?
Q X S V (object)

What did they **make** from the leftovers?
Q X S V (prepositional phrase)

Information Questions with modals

In questions with modals, use the same the auxiliary form for all subjects.

Who might know the answer?
Q/S X V (object)

Why must I **study** so much?
Q X S V

How many slices of pizza **can** Carlos **eat?**
Q   (object)   X S V

When could they **stop by?**
Q X S V

◼ 4-1 Question Intonation

Read the groups of words below. Rewrite them to make a correct English question. With a partner, practice reading aloud the full question. Be careful to use the correct intonation for English questions.

1. yesterday did what do work Kayla after?

   _____

2. going all are you I to fight and night?

   _____

3. when full was the Sayed arrived class?

   _____

4. calculator you me your please could lend?

   _____

5. if the closed where they go library is will?

   _____

6. for those I all books do this project need?

   _____

7. planning to they the early were concert go to?

   _____

8. come office should the professor's now Steve to?

   _____

◼ 4-2 Question Writing

A. Write three questions you might ask a classmate the first time you meet. Use present tense. Write both *Yes/No* and information questions.

   Example: What is your name? Where do you live? Do you like English class?

   1. _____

   2. _____

   3. _____

B. Write four questions to find out information about a classmate's son/daughter, sister/brother, or best friend (age, height, hobbies, physical appearance, etc.).

Example: How old is your son? How tall is he? What does he like to do?

4. _____

5. _____

6. _____

7. _____

C. Write four questions you might ask your English instructor. Use modals.

Example: What can I do to learn English? Could you help me write the paper? May I see my test scores?

8. _____

9. _____

10. _____

11. _____

D. Write four questions in the past tense to find out what happened in your last class.

Example: Did the professor give a test? Was it difficult? Did you hand in your homework?

12. _____

13. _____

14. _____

15. _____

E. Write four questions to find out what your friends are planning to do this weekend. Use present progressive or future tense.

Example: Are you going to go to the game? Will Hoshi work all weekend? Is Lisa watching a movie?

16. _____

17. _____

18. _____

19. _____

■ 4-3 Description of the Illustration

Look at the illustration. Use it to complete the activities.

A. With a partner, study the illustration carefully. Write ten questions in present tense about the illustration. Ask about who these people are, their activities, and the placement of objects in the room.

Example: Where is the computer?

1. _____

2. _____

3. _____

4. _____

5. _____

6. _____

7. _____

8. _____

9. _____

10. _____

B. Exchange your questions from Exercise A with another pair. Change your new questions into the past or future tense. Share them with the class.

4-4 Communicative Activity

Classroom Quiz Show

This game requires each student to write questions. Then the class is divided into two teams, and each team tries to answer the questions. Some of the questions will be easy to answer. They will be worth 10 points each. Others will be more difficult, and will be worth 30 or 50 points each. The goal is to earn the most points.

Directions

1. In your notebook, write an easy multiple choice *Yes/No* question with three answers. Only one answer is grammatically correct. This question is worth 10 points. It can be about anything, such as school, home life, hobbies, or politics.
   Example:

   10 points: Do you live in an apartment?

   a. Yes, I live.

   b. Yes, I do.

   c. Yes, I am.

   Now write two information questions worth 30 points each and two more worth 50 points each. The 50-point questions should be the most difficult.
   Example:

   30 points: What does Rafael do every evening?

   a. He was listening to music.

   b. He listens to music.

   c. He is going to listen to music.

   _50 points: While you and Aunt Sally _____ for new clothes, did you run into Uncle Fred at the mall?_

   a. shopped

   b. were shopping

   c. was shopping

2. Cut your questions into strips, so that each multiple choice question is on a different strip. Give these strips to your teacher. Your teacher will randomly select the questions and post them on the board. Then he/she will divide the class into two groups. A student from one team will choose a multiple choice question; if the student gets the answer correct, his/her team earns the specified points. Each team will take turns answering the questions. The team with the highest number of points wins the game.

▣ 4-5 Theme-based Discussion

Read each topic below. Make sure you understand the questions. Work in groups of four to discuss the first topic. Then, choose one person to report the group's answers to the class. Next, move to another group to discuss the next topic. Repeat this process until all the topics are discussed.

A. A reporter's main job is to ask people questions: What happened? When? Where? Why? What questions do you think a reporter should ask? Do you think there are questions that reporters should always avoid? Is there such a thing as a "dumb" question? Why do you think so?

B. Because you come from a different culture, people often ask you questions about your native country. Some of these questions are informational (*What is the capital of your country?*), and others are profound (*How do people from your country feel about global warming?*). Other questions, however, are just plain stupid. Make a list of the three stupidest questions that people have asked you about your country. Then share them with the others in your group.

1. _____

2. _____

3. _____

C. Suppose that you could interview anyone in the world—a political leader, a famous entertainer, a sports star, a writer. Choose one person, and in your notebook write 10 questions that you would ask him/her. Share your thoughts with the group.

■ 4-6 Grammar Practice

Read each answer below. Work with a partner to write two questions. Pay attention to the formulas. Look at the unit introduction if you need help remembering them. Use different verb tenses in the two questions.

1. **Question 1:** _Where is Jana?_

   Question 2: _Where were you last night when I got home?_

   Answer: In jail.

2. **Question 1:** _____

   Question 2: _____

   Answer: In the summer.

3. **Question 1:** _____

   Question 2: _____

   Answer: Tall and beautiful.

4. **Question 1:** _____

   Question 2: _____

   Answer: At six o'clock.

5. **Question 1:** _____

   Question 2: _____

   Answer: Pizza and a soda.

6. **Question 1:** _____

   Question 2: _____

   Answer: Professor Bergeron.

7. **Question 1:** _____

   Question 2: _____

   Answer: In 2002.

8. **Question 1:** _____

   Question 2: _____

   Answer: Three.

■ 4-7 Error Correction

Read the questions and answers below. There are mistakes in each one. The mistakes could be in subject–verb agreement, present, past or future tense forms or use, spelling, or missing words. Underline all the mistakes in each sentence, then write the sentence correctly.

1. What _doing_ Robert tomorrow at 3:30?

    What is Robert doing tomorrow at 3:30?

2. What time is the game start? I think it start at nine o'clock.

    _____

3. Where be they from? They from Colombia?

    _____

4. He is work in a pharmacy? He make a good salary.

    _____

5. Can you to tell me what time is?

    _____

6. Does Victoria and I had to go to school today?

    _____

7. Where were they shop this morning? At the grocery store and the mall.

    _____

8. You would lend me a book, please?

    _____

9. Why work Mosi two jobs? To pay for school.

    _____

10. When did go Chiang to class? When you sleep.

    _____

11. What weather like yesterday? It's cold?

    _____

12. Does'nt Horacio has a red car? No, he does. He's a green one.

    _____

13. Do he know the professor name?

    _____

▦ 4-8 Sentence Stems

Use the sentence stems below to write present, past, or future questions. Make sure the subjects and verbs agree and that you choose the appropriate form.

1. Who is _____ *your professor for chemistry?* _____

2. What does he _____

3. Why will you _____

4. When is Marco going to _____

5. How often does the teacher _____

6. How much did you _____

7. Whose baby is _____

8. Where are we _____

9. How many stars _____

10. What were you _____

▦ 4-9 Sentence Conclusions

Use the sentence conclusions below to write present, past, or future questions Make sure the subjects and verbs agree, and that you choose the appropriate form.

1. _____ *Did you pay the rent* _____ last month?

2. _____ next semester?

3. _____ right now?

4. _____ this winter?

5. _____ on Sunday?

6. _____ before we went home?

7. _____ to the beach?

8. _____ after the class ends?

9. _____ her for some advice?

10. _____ tomorrow evening?

■ 4-10 Communicative Activities

Workplaces: Imagine having a job in one of the following places: pet store, post office, department store, college registration office, airport, hospital, restaurant, or police station.

A. Think about what customers in each place would ask employees every day. Write two questions for each place on the lines below.

_____

_____

_____

_____

_____

_____

_____

_____

_____

_____

_____

_____

B. Your instructor will hand out slips of paper to each student with a workplace on it. Pretend that you work there. Answer other students' questions about your workplace.

Workplace: A pet store
Example questions: What kind of dog is that?

What do you feed him?

How much does he cost?

Does he have his shots?

■ 4-11 Grammar in Action

Impersonation

In this game, a student in the class will impersonate, or pretend to be, another student. The class will try to guess the student's secret identity by asking questions. For example, Mira stands in front of the class. One of her classmates, Juan, asks, "Are you a female?" Mira says, "No, I'm not." With this information, the class knows that Mira is impersonating a male classmate. Other students ask questions until they figure out who Mira is impersonating.

A. Before beginning the game, write some questions that you think will help you figure out who your classmates are impersonating. First write seven *Yes/No* questions.
Example: Are you from Colombia?

Yes/No **Questions**

1. _____

2. _____

3. _____

4. _____

5. _____

6. _____

7. _____

B. Now write seven information questions that require the "impersonator" to give more detailed answers.
Example: *What color is your hair?*

Information Questions

1. _____

2. _____

3. _____

4. _____

5. _____

6. _____

7. _____

C. Now you are ready to begin the game. Your teacher will ask a student to come to the front of the room and impersonate another classmate. The class will alternate between *Yes/No* and information questions to try to guess the identity.

Look at the photograph. Use it to complete the activities below with a partner.

A. Imagine that the boy's parents are showing you the picture. In your notebook, write 10 questions about it. Try to use at least two different tenses.

B. Exchange notebooks with a partner. Answer your partner's questions in his/her notebook. Use full sentences. Be careful to answer in the same tense as the question. When you are finished, return your partner's notebook.

C. Read your partner's answers to the questions you wrote. Use them to write a paragraph about the photographs. Again, try to use at least two of the tenses you have learned so far.

4-13 The Writing Page

A. On the lines below, write a paragraph about your future plans. Five years from now, where will you be? What will you be doing? Will you be married? Have a family? Write at least six sentences.

_____

_____

_____

_____

_____

_____

_____

B. Do you know the English expression "playing devil's advocate"? It means to look at potential problems in a plan in order to solve them or change the plan. Show your paragraph from Exercise A to a partner. On the lines below, write "devil's advocate" questions about your partner's paragraph. For example, if your partner writes that he wants to be a millionaire in five years, you could write "How will you save a million dollars in five years?" Write as many problem-solving questions as you can.

_____

_____

_____

_____

_____

_____

_____

C Read your partner's questions from Exercise B. Write answers or changes to your plan in your notebook.

■ 4-14 Unit Review

Directed Writing

Task: Write a three-paragraph essay about a trip through time.

Prewriting

You have a time machine and can visit different times and places. You could choose to go back into the past—or forward into the future—and then return to the present. Of course, you want to learn about the people living in these different time periods and write a report when you return home. What do you want to learn about? Food? Transportation? Medicine? Work? Government? What questions will you ask? In your notebook, make notes about your destinations for your time trip and the questions you might ask. Use a chart like the one below.

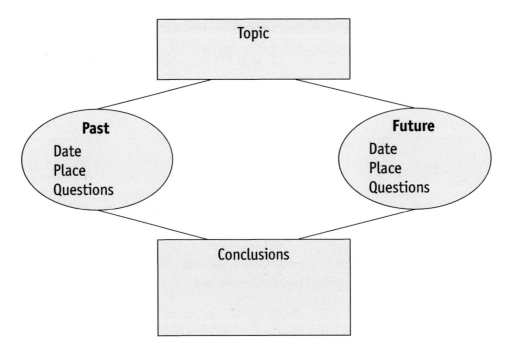

First Draft

Write a first draft of your essay. Use your chart and notes to organize your ideas as you write. Check that your first paragraph introduces the purpose for your time trip into the past and the questions you would ask. Your second paragraph describes your trip into the future, including questions. Make sure that your third paragraph gives a conclusion about what you learned from your time trips. Use as many different verb tenses in the questions as you can. Ask both *Yes/No* questions and information questions.

> **Model**
>
> In my time machine, I want to learn about past and future transportation. My first stop is in the year 1492 with the Santa Maria on its return trip to Spain. I'll ask Christopher Columbus, "Did you enjoy this trip? What will you do differently on your next trip? What was the most difficult part about this trip? Why did you leave some of your men in the New World?" I'm sure Christopher Columbus will have plenty of time to answer these questions. If there is time, I'll also ask some of the sailors on his ship the same questions...
>
> My next stop is in the year 2505. Will the world be different? I think so. I'll try to go to a city to see the types of transportation. I'll ask the first friendly person, "How do you travel from city to city? Do people still use petroleum for fuels?...
>
> Finally, I'll arrive home. Everyone will want to know what I learned on my trip...

Revision

Read through your essay and check for correct word order in questions, correct usage of question words and auxiliary verbs, clear main idea and details, and correct spelling and punctuation. Share your essay with a partner. Your partner should be able to answer the following questions about your essay:

- Where and when did you travel in your time machine?
- What questions did you ask?
- Did you use correct word order in the questions?
- Did you use different question words?
- Do you have any errors in spelling or punctuation?
- Does the essay need any more information?

Final Draft

Make any changes or additions that are needed in your essay. Then write or type a final copy. You may want to include your final essay in a portfolio of your writing.

Evaluation

Your teacher will grade your essay. You will be evaluated on:

- clarity of ideas and level of supporting detail in your essay;
- use of correct word order and verb forms in questions; and
- use of different tenses in questions.

Unit 5

Present Perfect and Present Perfect Progressive

The Present Perfect Tense: *Unfinished Business*

Although the name says "present" perfect tense, this tense describes conditions or actions from the *past* that continue into the *present*. In contrast to the simple past (a finished condition or action), the present perfect describes conditions or actions related and important to the present.

> We **were** friends a long time ago. (The past tense implies that you aren't friends now; the friendship ended.)
> We **have been** friends for 20 years. (The present perfect tense implies that you still are friends in the present.)

Using the Present Perfect Tense

The present perfect tense is used in the following situations:

1. **to express conditions and actions that happened over a period of time (up to and including the present) without stating a specific time period**
   Have you **eaten** frog's legs?
   My brother **has fallen** asleep at the wheel several times.
   They **have** never **been** to Africa.

2. **to express an experience within a set period of time**
   The period of time can be set by a calendar (a week, two months, a five-year plan), by seasonal time (Christmas season, summer vacation, fall) or by an activity (the baseball playoffs, Macy's winter sale, etc.). Within this time, certain actions are expected to happen or might happen. Words and phrases such as *already, yet, still,* and *so far* are used with present perfect to indicate a time period. For more on these words, see the Appendix before you begin the activities.

3. **in expressions with *for* and *since***
   For more on these expressions, see the Appendix before you begin the activities.

Forming the Present Perfect Tense

Affirmative Statements
Use *have/has* + the past participle. For regular verbs, the past participle has the same form as the past tense. There is a list of the past participles of irregular verbs on page 200. The best way to learn irregular forms is to use them as often as you can.
Past: I **called** my sister in Colorado yesterday.   Present perfect: I **have called** her every week since May.

Past:	Present Perfect:
I **drove** a Honda last year.	I **have** (I've) always **driven** Hondas.
Eun Ju **ate** raw fish for dinner.	Manolo **has** (Manolo's) never **eaten** raw fish.
I **went out** with Kenji yesterday.	You **have** (You've) **gone out** with him before.

Negative Statements
I **have not (haven't) visited** Ireland before.   We **have not (haven't) seen** Ana for several days.   You **have not (haven't) written** your paper yet.   You (plural) **have not (haven't) eaten** dinner.   He/She **has not (hasn't) gone** to school this week.   They **have not (haven't) brought** in the mail today.

When asking a question with *ever*, you are asking about a person's entire life. If they have done something one time, they will answer *Yes*. Questions without *ever* refer to actions and conditions close to the present.

Have I ever **met** them before? Yes, you **have.**/No, you **have not (haven't).**

Have you ever **traveled** to Saudi Arabia? Yes, I **have.**/No, I **have not (haven't).**

Has he/she **finished** dinner? Yes, he/she **has.**/No, he/she **has not (hasn't).**

Have we ever **eaten** at this restaurant? Yes, we **have.**/No, we **have not (haven't).**

Have you (plural) **cleaned** the kitchen? Yes, we **have.**/No, we **have not (haven't).**

Have they ever **seen** a museum? Yes, they **have.**/No, they **have not (haven't).**

Note: The past participle is not used in short answers.

Information Questions

Information questions follow the same pattern as *Yes/No* questions but begin with a question word.

Who has read today's assignment?	Milena has.
What have you **done?**	I spilled the milk.
When have I **been** late?	Last week.
Why have we **waited** so long for a table?	Because the restaurant is new.
Where have they **been?**	In Ecuador.

The Present Perfect Progressive Tense: *What Has Been Going On?*

The present perfect progressive expresses one continuous action that is often happening close to the present time.

Using the Present Perfect Progressive Tense

There are three patterns that can use either the present perfect or the present perfect progressive tense and mean the same thing in either tense.

1. **in expressions with *for* and *since***

   Phrases with *for* and phrases and clauses with *since* can show how long a continuous action has lasted.

   I **have been reading (have read)** the same page **for over an hour.**

   We **have been living (have lived)** in this apartment **since 1998.**

2. **to express continuous or single actions very close to the present, with *recently, lately,* and *just***

   Bob **has been feeling** much better **lately.**

   Ludmilla **has recently visited** Boston.

   Aunt Maudie **has just painted** the bookshelf, so please don't touch it.

3. **to express a condition or long-term habitual action**

   I **have been living** in New Jersey **since my daughter was born.**

   Karen **has been practicing for more than five years.**

   They **have been going** to baseball's opening day every season **since 1999.**

Forming the Present Perfect Progressive Tense

Use *have/has* + *been* + the present participle (base verb + *-ing*). Questions in the present perfect progressive follow the same pattern as present perfect.

I **have been going** to school for three weeks.

Have you **been staying up** late?

He/She **hasn't been feeling** well today.

We **have been listening** to the game on the radio.

How long **have** you **been dancing?**

They **have been attending** the school meetings.

Differences in Meaning between Present Perfect and Present Perfect Progressive

As noted on page 73, sometimes the present perfect and the present perfect progressive tenses can mean the same thing. Other times, each tense has a different meaning.

The present perfect tense expresses repeated actions.
Senay **has talked** to Ray three times about his bad attitude.
Elizabeta **has donated** blood four times this year.

The present perfect progressive tense expresses one long, continuous action that is often happening close to the present time.
Almi **has been talking** on the phone to her fiancé in Peru for more than an hour.
"Someone **has been sleeping** in my bed," said the baby bear to Goldilocks.

■ 5-1 Grammar Discussion

Read each pair of sentences below. In each pair, one sentence uses present perfect, and the other present perfect progressive. Work with a partner to decide how the meanings of the sentences are different. Share your answers with the class.

A1. I haven't watched that show before.
A2. I haven't been watching that show.

B1. Keith has been going to the hospital this week.
B2. Keith has gone to the hospital this week.

C1. Jorge and Ray have written their paper.
C2. Jorge and Ray have been writing their paper.

D1. Have you and Sheila been shopping?
D2. Have you and Sheila shopped?

E1. We have been seeing a therapist.
E2. We have seen a therapist.

F1. What has Kayla been doing at school?
F2. What has Kayla done at school?

G1. You and Han haven't been eating enough.
G2. You and Han haven't eaten enough.

■ 5-2 Sentence Writing

Conditions or actions over a period of time

A. Use the present perfect tense to write three sentences about places you have never been but would like to go.
   Example: I have never been to Antarctica, but I would love to go there.

1. _____

2. _____

3. _____

B. Use the present perfect tense to write three sentences about something that you have never eaten or drunk.
Example: I have never eaten Ethiopian food.

4. _____

5. _____

6. _____

With *for* and *since*

C. Use the present perfect tense to write three sentences about what you have done since the beginning of the semester.
Example: I have studied every Thursday since the beginning of the semester.

7. _____

8. _____

9. _____

Actions within a specific time period with *yet*

D. This month has been very busy. Using the present perfect tense, write three negative sentences about things you haven't done yet. Review the information on *yet* in the Appendix if needed.
Example: I haven't gone to the grocery store yet this month.

10. _____

11. _____

12. _____

Continuous actions beginning at a certain point

E. Use the present perfect progressive tense to write two sentences about what you have been doing since you came to the United States.
Example: I've been going to English classes three times a week.

13. _____

14. _____

F. Use the present perfect progressive tense to write two sentences about what you have been doing lately in class.
Example: Lately, we have been studying present perfect progressive.

15. _____

16. _____

■ 5-3 Description of the Illustration

Look at the illustration below. Use it to complete the activities.

A. Have you ever been really afraid of something? Describe the illustration. What's going on here in the picture? What is the man afraid of? Write at least 10 sentences in your notebook to tell the story of the "Terrified Man." Use present perfect or present perfect progressive if you can.

B. In your notebook, write at least 10 sentences describing an incident in your life when you were really afraid of something. Your topic sentence might be: "I have always been afraid of _____, and I will tell you a story to explain why." Use present perfect to write affirmative and negative sentences.

■ 5-4 Communicative Activity: *The Good Angel or the Bad Angel*

A. Take a survey of your classmates to find out some of their deepest desires secret wishes, both good and bad. You will ask classmates about four categories of desires: physical–good; physical–bad; emotional–good; emotional–bad. Here are some examples for each category:

> Physical–Bad: She has often wanted to make her boyfriend be quiet.
> Physical–Good: He has always wanted to give massages to people in pain.
> Emotional–Bad: He has been dying to tell everyone his cousin's secret.
> Emotional–Good: She has decided to smile at everyone she sees today.

B. Talk with your classmates. Ask three different students about each category.
   Example: Student A: *What is something bad (physical) that you have wanted to do?*
   Student B: *I have often wanted to make my boyfriend be quiet.*

Now write each classmate's answer in the appropriate category below.

PHYSICAL–BAD

1. _____

_____

2. _____

_____

3. _____

_____

PHYSICAL–GOOD

1. _____

_____

2. _____

_____

3. _____

_____

EMOTIONAL–BAD

1. _____

_____

2. _____

_____

3. _____

_____

EMOTIONAL–GOOD

1. _____

_____

2. _____

_____

3. _____

_____

C. Look at the sentences you wrote about your classmates. Are the most memorable examples in the **GOOD** or the **BAD** category? Are they in the **PHYSICAL** or the **EMOTIONAL** category? Are some of the desires very similar? Are there any particular desires that you would like to see come true? Discuss these questions with the class.

■ 5-5 Theme-based Discussion

Read each topic below. Make sure you understand the questions. Work in groups of four to discuss the first topic. Then choose one person to report the group's answers to the class. Next, move to another group to discuss the next topic. Repeat this process until all the topics are discussed.

A. Think about the family that you grew up in. Describe its personality by figuring out who has always been the leader, the complainer, the negotiator, the stubborn resistor, the comic, the philosopher, the charmer, the bully, and so on. Does your class also have a personality? Can you describe that personality in the same way?

B. Do buildings ever affect the way you feel about yourself while you are in them? How do the buildings at your college sometimes make you feel? How do the buildings in your town make you feel?

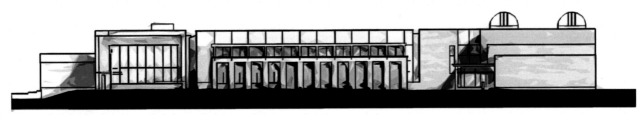

Technology Building, Bergen Community College, Paramus, New Jersey
Ronald Schmidt Associates and Fred Rosen Associates, Architects

C. Are you a planner? Do you have a calendar that you use to plan weeks ahead? Or are you spontaneous—someone who lives only in the moment? After you decide which you are, think of a relationship you have with someone who is the opposite way. How does that relationship work out? What are some of the techniques you each use so that you won't get on each other's nerves?

Day 1	Breakfast with Angelica (8:00)
	Dinner with Michael (7:30)
Day 2	Pick up dry cleaning
	Finish reading Chapter 12
Day 3	Modern Art Museum with Shin (12:00)
	Coffee with Paul (3:00)
	Dinner with the Thompsons (7:00)

■ 5-6 Communicative Activity: Creative Listings

Too often people ignore their own accomplishments and positive achievements. But you have already done so much in your life. Walk around the class, asking your classmates questions about things they have done. Write their names and their responses on the lines below. Write three responses to each question. Then write your own response on the last line. Then, be ready to participate in a classroom discussion. Use the present perfect in your questions and discussion.

Example: You: What countries have you visited?
      Alex: I have visited Canada.

Countries visited

1. _Alex: Canada_ _____

2. _____

3. _____

4. _____

Languages studied

1. _____

2. _____

3. _____

4. _____

Houses lived in

1. _____

2. _____

3. _____

4. _____

Cities and countries lived in

1. _____

2. _____

3. _____

4. _____

Schools attended

1. _____

2. _____

3. _____

4. _____

Places visited in the United States

1. _____

2. _____

3. _____

4. _____

**Countries where friends/
classmates come from**

1. _____

2. _____

3. _____

4. _____

**Religions of people
in your class**

1. _____

2. _____

3. _____

4. _____

■ 5-7 Error Correction

The <u>underlined</u> verbs in the story below are in the wrong tense and need to be corrected. With a partner, decide what the correct tense and form for each verb should be. Then rewrite the story correctly.

Maria

Maria is a professional photographer. When she **(1)** <u>come</u> here five years ago from France, she **(2)** <u>doesn't know</u> a lot about photography. But she **(3)** <u>was studying</u> at a famous school in San Francisco after she **(4)** <u>has arrived</u> in this country. Now Maria's specialty is wildlife. She **(5)** <u>is taking</u> photographs of wild animals. She **(6)** <u>sold</u> many of her pictures to different magazines since she **(7)** <u>has started</u> doing this work. So far, she **(8)** <u>traveled</u> to Africa and Brazil, but she **(9)** <u>doesn't visit</u> India yet. Several times, she **(10)** <u>had</u> problems doing this kind of work. For example, a large animal almost **(11)** <u>has killed</u> her in Africa. Clearly, Maria **(12)** <u>lived</u> an exciting life.

Right now, Maria **(13)** <u>works</u> on a project for *National Geographic Magazine*. For several weeks, she **(14)** <u>takes</u> pictures of bears in the Rocky Mountains. Last week, while she **(15)** <u>studied</u> a mother bear with her babies, she **(16)** <u>sees</u> several snakes, so she **(17)** <u>takes</u> some pictures of them, too. As soon as Maria **(18)** <u>finished</u> her project on the bears, she **(19)** <u>go</u> back to Africa to photograph elephants.

_____

_____

_____

_____

_____

_____

_____

_____

_____

_____

_____

_____

5-8 Sentence Frames

Use the sentence stems and conclusions below to write statements and questions using present perfect or present perfect progressive tense. Make sure the subjects and verbs agree and that you choose the appropriate tense.

1. She _____ *has* _____ enjoyed college.

2. Lately, I _____ .

3. _____ you _____ yet?

4. She _____ four or five times this month.

5. They _____ just _____ , so don't _____ .

6. What _____ recently?

7. Your brother _____ or twice, hasn't he?

8. She _____ since noon.

9. Have _____ ever _____ ?

10. Have they _____ ?

11. Ever since she _____ , she _____ .

12. Has Steven ever _____ ?

13. For a year, we _____ .

14. You _____ since last December.

15. I _____ six books this semester.

16. Tomas and Elena _____ every day.

17. Jun and Wendy _____ for a month.

18. They still _____ .

■ 5-9 Grammar in Action

Write short paragraphs for each topic. Be aware that when you use the past tense, you are expressing a specific period of time, and when you use the present perfect (progressive) tense, you are focusing on the action or condition without stating a specific period of time. When you are finished, share your paragraphs with a partner.

A. You have probably lived with or near your family most of your life. Discuss how your family has influenced your life, either positively or negatively.

_____

_____

_____

_____

_____

_____

_____

B. Think about your life goals—the accomplishments or events that you expect to happen in your life. Which goals have you already reached, and which ones haven't you reached yet?

_____

_____

_____

_____

_____

_____

_____

C. Have you ever felt stuck in a place? Is that true now? The place might be a city, town, country, college, or company. It might be an emotional place such as a relationship, marriage, or parental role. Discuss how you feel trapped and how long you have felt this way.

_____

_____

_____

_____

_____

_____

_____

D. Write about what you have learned in grammar, reading, writing, and listening/speaking this semester. Then tell what you haven't studied yet so far.

_____

_____

_____

_____

_____

_____

_____

5-10 The Writing Page

A. Complete the story below. The first and last sentences have been provided. Use present perfect and present perfect progressive, along with the words below, to write sentences that lead logically to the concluding sentence.

Story 1

yet	for (+phrase)	since (+clause)
four or five times	never	lately

Bill stared at the dark-haired beauty standing in the other line in the cafeteria.

_____

_____

_____

_____

_____

_____

_____

_____

He wanted to rush over and kiss her, but he didn't, of course.

B. Complete the next story in your notebook. As in Exercise A, use present perfect and present perfect progressive if you can, along with the words below. The first and last sentences have been provided.

Story 2

still	many times	already
since (+phrase)	recently	so far

First sentence:
Lucia was thrilled when she saw the full-length Burberry wool coat in the store window.

Last sentence:
As she walked out the door, she told herself that she was a woman of restraint and honor.

5-11 Description of the Photograph

Look at the photograph below. Use it to complete the activities.

A. With a partner, study the photograph. In your notebook, write seven affirmative and negative sentences to describe what you think has been going on. Use present perfect progressive.
Example: The woman has been waiting a long time.

B. How have you been feeling lately? In your notebook, describe your feelings and then explain what has been going on in your life to make you feel that way. Use present perfect and present perfect progressive if you can.

■ 5-12 Unit Review

Directed Writing

Task: Write a three-paragraph essay about what you have done to get your perfect job.

Prewriting

You are applying for your perfect job. Now you need to write about why you should get this job. What have you been doing to prepare for this particular type of job? What courses have you taken? What skills have you developed? What kind of work have you already done? How long did you work at your last job? In your notebook, make notes about your experience and the skills that are needed for this perfect job. Use a chart like the one below.

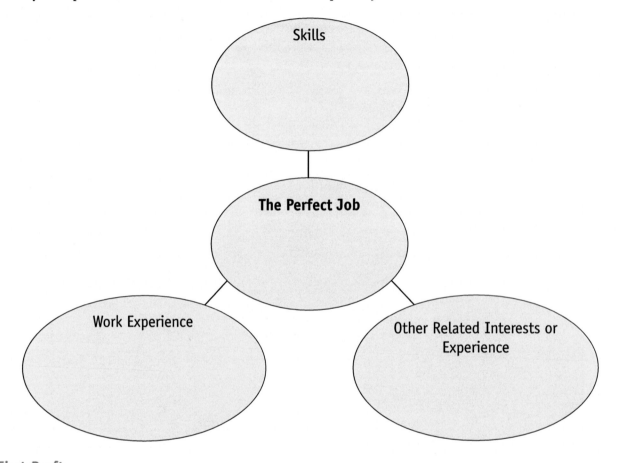

First Draft

Write a first draft of your essay. Use your chart and notes to organize your ideas as you write. Check that your first paragraph introduces the job and why you want it. Use the second paragraph to describe specific skills and experience you have had. Make sure that your third paragraph gives a conclusion why you should get the job. Use present perfect and present perfect progressive with appropriate time expressions. Write both affirmative and negative sentences.

> **Model**   Since I was five years old, I have always wanted to be a photographer. I have been taking photos of sports for twelve years now. I believe I will be a great sports photographer...
>
> I received my first camera when I was eight years old, and I have been taking pictures of my school's sports events since 1998. I've learned a lot...
>
> This job would be perfect for me because I love sports and I love to show the action and emotions of the athletes. I've already had some of my photos published in the local newspaper...

Revision

Read through your essay and check for correct use and form of present perfect and present perfect progressive, use of time expressions, clear main idea and details, and correct spelling and punctuation. Share your essay with a partner. Your partner should be able to answer the following questions about your essay:

- What job do you want?
- What experience have you had?
- What have you studied to prepare for this job?
- Did you use the present perfect and/or present perfect progressive?
- Did you use different time expressions?
- Do you have any errors in spelling or punctuation?
- Does the essay need any more information?

Final Draft

Make any changes or additions that are needed in your essay. Then write or type a final copy. You may want to include your final essay in a portfolio of your writing.

Evaluation

Your teacher will grade your essay. You will be evaluated on:

- clarity of ideas and level of supporting detail in your essay;
- use of present perfect and present perfect progressive; and
- use of different time expressions.

Unit 6

Modals of Ability, Possibility, Probability, and Advice

Modals add special meaning to the verbs that follow them. They are used for five special purposes; to express ability, permission, advice, possibility, and probability. You will study modals of necessity and prohibition in Unit 7.

Different types of modals are used in each of the following situations:

1. **to talk about ability**

   I **can't drive** to work this week. My car's being repaired.

   Vicki and Matthew **are able to walk** to school. It's close by.

   She **could speak** Korean fluently three years ago.

   They **couldn't get** through because the road was closed.

   For ability in the present, use *can/can't* or *be able to* + the base form of the verb. Use *could* or *couldn't* for ability in the past.

2. **to ask or give permission**

   May I **borrow** your notebook? Yes, you **may**.

   Would you please **drive** my sister to the game? No, I **won't**.

   Could they pick us up from the airport? I think they **can**.

   The modals of permission include *may, can, could, would*, and *will*. Use the modal + the base form of the verb.

3. **to give advice**

   I'm confused. **Should** I **talk** with the professor?

   He **ought to pay** his rent on time.

   We **shouldn't go** to Ohio this weekend. It might snow.

   Use *should/shouldn't* + the base form of the verb or *ought to* + the base form of the verb for advice in the present or future. *Should* is more common than *ought to*.

4. **to discuss possibility**

   I **might be** late for class tomorrow.

   You **may not finish** your reading in time.

   Rhonda and William **could get married** next month.

   Use *may, might*, or *could* + the base form for possibility in the present or future.

5. **to discuss probability or a high degree of certainty**

   You **must be** Aldo's new girlfriend. (My son told me that you were a tall, beautiful woman.)

   Heddie **must be** exhausted after her trip. (The flight took 22 hours.)

   We **must be** early. (No one else is here.)

   Use *must* + the base form of the verb for probability or high degree of certainty in the present.

Modals with Present Perfect

Modals themselves do not have a tense. To discuss ability, permission, advice, possibility, or probability about past actions, English speakers often use present perfect. Using present perfect implies that the past action still has some effect on the present time.

1. **to talk about ability**
   I **couldn't have driven** to school last week. My car was in the shop. (I was unable to drive.)
   Susan **could have gone** to Asia in May. (She had the ability, but didn't go.)

2. **to ask or give permission**
   Could they **have picked** us **up** from the airport? (The time to pick us up has passed.)

3. **to give advice**
   Tony **should have taken** the job. (But he didn't.)
   We **shouldn't have bought** a new computer. (But we did, and now we're broke.)

4. **to discuss possibility**
   I **might have been** late for class if I hadn't woken up.
   You **may have written** a very interesting thesis.
   We **could have won** the lottery, but I didn't buy a ticket.

5. **to discuss probability or high degree of certainty**
   This **must have been** the pie Dad made for dinner. (There are only crumbs left.)
   Pyotr **must have eaten** the whole thing. (He was the only one at home this afternoon.)

Different Kinds of Modals

1. *be able to* is a modal of ability, similar to *can* and *could*. It is usually used for emphasis or in more formal speech or writing. Unlike most modals, *be able to* does change form and tense.
   I **haven't been able to come** to class; my leg is broken.
   They **were able to visit** before the holidays, even though they couldn't come to the party.

2. *had better* is a modal of advice, similar to *should* and *ought to*. It is usually heard in casual speech as a contraction.
   We**'d better go** in the house. There's a storm coming.
   You**'d better not bother** the dog. He might bite.

In spoken English, modals are sometimes stressed, and in some cases the pronunciation is reduced.

Modals and Stress

In affirmative statements, modals are unstressed. In negative statements, there is stress on both the negative modals and the base verbs.

can vs. can't	I can <u>snowboard</u>, but I <u>can't ski</u>.
could vs. couldn't	We could <u>go</u> to the movies tonight.
	Too bad Marcos <u>couldn't come</u> with us.

Reduced Forms of Modals

In informal speech, not all the letters in the modals are pronounced distinctly. For example:

can/can't	[kən] [kænt]
couldn't	[kʊdnt]
ought to	[ɔtə]

In questions with modals, the subject pronoun you may be combined with the modals. Together, they may sound like one word. For example:

will you	[wilyə]	could've	[kʊdə]
can you	[kænyə]	should've	[ʃʊdə]
would you	[wʊdʒə]		
could you	[kʊdʒə]		

■ 6-1 **Pronunciation**

Read the questions in Column A. How would you respond? Write the letter of the correct response from Column B. Then practice the questions and answers with a partner.

Column A	Column B
_____F_____ 1. How do I get to Springfield?	**A.** Sorry, I [kænt]. I hurt my back yesterday.
_____ 2. [kænyə] tell me the time?	**B.** Sure, here you are.
_____ 3. Did you do the homework?	**C.** Well, I [kən] write programs and use Photoshop®.
_____ 4. What classes [wilyə] take next year?	**D.** I don't know yet. I haven't decided.
_____ 5. [wʊdʒə] pass me the salt?	**E.** They're on your head.
_____ 6. I [kænt] find my glasses.	**F.** You [ɔtə] take Bus 24.
_____ 7. [kʊdʒə] help me lift this box?	**G.** No, I [kʊdnt]. I left my book in the classroom.
_____ 8. What skills do you have?	**H.** It's 10:25.

▪ 6-2 Sentence Writing

Modals

Ability

A. Use modals of ability and present perfect tense to write three sentences about things you could have done last year, but didn't.
Example: I could have been on the Dean's list, but I got a C in History.

1. _____

2. _____

3. _____

Permission

B. Use modals of permission to write two questions you want to ask your professor about your class.
Example: Could you tell me my grade? Would you look at the outline for my paper?

4. _____

5. _____

Advice

C. Your brother went to the same college as his girlfriend. Now they aren't together, and he's unhappy. Use modals of advice and present perfect tense to write two sentences about what he should have done differently.
Example: He should have chosen his own college. He ought to have talked to his girlfriend about it.

6. _____

7. _____

Possibility

D. Use modals of possibility to write two sentences about what you might do during Winter Break. Write at least one negative sentence.
Example: I might not go home. I may stay at school with my roommate.

8. _____

9. _____

Probability or High Degree of Certainty

E. Your roommate had a party last night. The next day, you come home, and your apartment is a mess. Use a modal of probability to write two sentences about what must have happened.
Example: My roommate must have invited a lot of people. Everyone must have had a good time.

10. _____

11. _____

■ 6-3 Description of the Illustration

Look at the illustration below. Use it to complete the activities.

A. Study the illustration with a partner. Use modals of possibility to write five sentences explaining why the people in the picture (the cashier, the customer, the people in line, the clerks) might be frustrated, and what problem they might be facing.

Example: The cashier might be frustrated because the register is broken.

1. _____

2. _____

3. _____

4. _____

5. _____

B. Now use modals of possibility to write five sentences about how the problems you listed in Exercise A could be solved.

Example: The cashier could take the customer to another register.

6. _____

7. _____

8. _____

9. _____

10. _____

C. Share your sentences from Exercise A and Exercise B with the class. Does anyone have other suggestions to solve the problems you listed?

6-4 Communicative Activity: Class Radio Show

A. Your class has been asked to prepare a one-hour radio show. Read through the list of tasks in the table below. With your partner, decide who is able to do each of the tasks. (Use modals of ability: *can, could.*) Write their names in the table. For example:

Example: You: Olga can introduce the songs because she knows a lot about music.

              Partner: Everyone could bring in files. Then we'll have a big list of songs that we can use.

Tasks	Name(s) and Reasons
• bring in music files	
• select music	
• arrange a play list	
• operate the computer	
• introduce the songs	
• tell jokes	
• watch the time	

B. Discuss with your partner some other possible ideas for the radio program. Use modals of possibility (*may, might, could*). Write your ideas on the lines below.

Example: You: We could talk about international news.

              Partner: Good idea. We also might announce the concert and sports events that are happening this weekend.

_____

_____

_____

C. You and your partner need to convince the rest of the class about your choices. Give some advice about the program. Use modals for advice (*should, ought to*). Write your ideas on the lines below.

Example: You: We should have a special theme for the program.

              Partner: We ought to have people call with requests for songs.

_____

_____

_____

■ 6-5 Theme-based Discussion

Read each topic below. The topics for discussion in this unit are controversial issues. Make sure you understand the questions. Work in groups of four to discuss the first topic. Provide support for your opinion. It is very important to respect the right of the other members of your group to hold a different opinion from your own. Then choose one person to report the group's answers to the class. Next move to another group to discuss the next topic. Repeat this process until all the topics are discussed.

A. The use of some drugs is against the law in the United States. There is often a great deal of discussion, though, on how to punish people who buy and use these drugs. Should they be sent to jail? Or should they be put in a hospital or rehabilitation clinic? Discuss the issue of punishing drug users. Focus on the pros and cons of each solution.

B. Another topic of recent debate is whether it should be legal for two members of the same sex to get married or have the same legal protections as married couples have. This is a good example of how many laws in the United States vary from state to state. How do you feel about the issue? Give reasons to support your opinion.

C. There are homeless people in every city in America. Whose responsibility is it to take care of them? Should the city government (and thus the taxpayers) provide food, shelter, and clothing for the homeless population of its town? Or should homeless people be encouraged (or forced) to work for the food and shelter they receive?

■ 6-6 Communicative Activity

A. Think about a relationship you had with someone who broke a promise to you or disappointed you in some way. It can be any type of relationship—family, romantic, work-related, or financial. It can be a relationship with a friend, a neighbor, or a co-worker. Write five sentences about how this person disappointed you.

_____

_____

_____

_____

_____

_____

_____

_____

B. Tell a partner about the person who disappointed you. Discuss what the person did. Make sure you answer the following questions:

What could the person do to gain your forgiveness?
Example: She could apologize for spilling coffee on my coat.

What should this person do?
Example: She should offer to have my coat cleaned. I may not accept, but she should offer.

6-7 Cloze

A. Read the story and write a modal in each blank. Review the unit introduction if you need help. You will use some of the modals more than once.

Statues of Chac Mool, a strange human figure, are found in Toltec temples in Mexico and Central America. Carlos Fuentes wrote a story about a man, Filiberto, who bought a Chac Mool statue. A friend was reading Filiberto's journal.

Sunday: My friend Pepe knows that I collect statues. He said that I **(1)** _ought to_ look at a statue of Chac Mool in a little antique shop. The stone doesn't look so old, so the statue **(2)** _____ not be authentic. The shopkeeper insists that it is. I suppose it **(3)** _____ be real, but I doubt it. I bought it anyway and moved it back to my house. It's in the basement right now, but it really **(4)** _____ be displayed in the sunlight.

Monday: You **(5)** _____ have seen the mess in the basement. The water pipes broke last night. I **(6)** _____ have left the water running in the kitchen, and now the basement is full of water. The statue is all right, but I **(7)** _____ not get to work on time because the plumbers **(8)** _____ not get here right away.

Wednesday: I **(9)** _____ sleep much last night. I heard some strange sounds, and the pipes broke again. In addition, it rained last night, and all the rainwater got into the basement!

Thursday: I **(10)** _____ have to sell the house if these problems continue. I **(11)** _____ scrape moss off Chac Mool because the basement is so damp. I really **(12)** _____ move the statue upstairs.

Friday: Last night Chac Mool came into my bedroom! **(13)** _____ anybody help me? I **(14)** _____ believe all of this...

Saturday: I **(15)** _____ continue living in this house with all the water. I **(16)** _____ get out of here now! The journal ended there. The friend went to Filiberto's house. He saw a strange-looking yellow Indian at the door...

B. What do you think happened to Filiberto? What do you think Filiberto should have done?

■ 6-8 Grammar in Action

A. Read each situation below with a partner. After each situation, there are three sentences of advice. Some of the advice is good, and some of the advice is bad. Read each sentence with a partner and decide whether it is GOOD advice or BAD advice. Circle your answers.

Situation 1: I have a daughter at a university in Missouri. She is a freshman. In high school, she got her best grades in literature and history. Now she is getting her best grades in economics.

GOOD   BAD   **1.** She should continue studying economics.

GOOD   BAD   **2.** She should talk to her advisor about what courses to take next year.

GOOD   BAD   **3.** She should stop studying economics and take only history courses.

Situation 2: I have a friend who got a dog last year. He travels a lot on business, but he is talking about getting another dog.

GOOD   BAD   **4.** He shouldn't get another dog if he is going to travel a lot.

GOOD   BAD   **5.** He should get a different job that doesn't require travel.

GOOD   BAD   **6.** He should get another dog so that the two dogs could keep each other company while he's traveling.

Situation 3: My best friend is overweight and needs to lose about 80 pounds. She wants to go on a low-carb diet because she has heard that it works.

GOOD   BAD   **7.** She should eat a lot of pasta so that she feels full.

GOOD   BAD   **8.** To lose the weight quickly, she shouldn't eat anything at all for the first four days.

GOOD   BAD   **9.** She should consult her doctor before starting the diet.

B. Now choose one of the situations above. Write a paragraph in your notebook giving your own advice. You can use the sentences above, but make sure to change any bad advice to a negative sentence. When you are finished, share your advice with the class.

■ 6-9 Error Correction

Read the sentences below. Each sentence has at least one mistake. The mistakes could be in verb form, subject–verb agreement, or choice of modal. Underline all the mistakes in each sentence, then write the sentence correctly.

1. If you want to get a raise, <u>you better to start</u> working harder.

    If you want to get a raise, you'd better start working harder.

2. May you please turn down the radio? I can concentrate with that classical music.

    _____

3. This weekend, I maybe go to the beach, or I could to go to the museum.

    _____

4. Could I speaking with Sigmund?

    _____

5. Julie is come from Korea. She may to speak Korean.

    _____

6. Might be Gultekin from Turkey or from Jordan. I'm not sure.

    _____

7. You shouldn't be quiet about the broken vase. Dad be very angry.

    _____

8. My brother work in an appliance store, so I could to get a discount on a microwave.

    _____

9. Ty and Mohammed can have been at the movies.

    _____

10. Sascha may to ask the professor.

    _____

11. Will I can see the dress?

    _____

12. We have better to leave early; it's snowing.

    _____

■ 6-10 Sentence Stems

Use the sentence stems below to write true statements using modals. Write both affirmative and negative sentences.

1. People on a diet *might not eat enough food.* _____

2. Teachers _____

3. Good students _____

4. I hate being late. Next time, _____

5. Police officers _____

6. Doctors _____

7. Rich people _____

8. Michelle isn't going out tonight. She _____

9. I'm not sure what I'll do for vacation next summer. I _____

10. Be careful. You _____

■ 6-11 Sentence Conclusions

Use the sentence conclusions below to write statements of advice, ability, possibility, probability, and permission using modals. Write both affirmative and negative statements.

1. _____ *You shouldn't* _____ smoke in the classroom.

2. _____ play soccer in the dining room with all these crystal glasses.

3. _____ go to the movies tonight because I have to study.

4. _____ call her to apologize.

5. _____ run five miles.

6. _____ lend me your dictionary for a minute, please.

7. _____ be from Iran. Her whole family lives in Teheran.

8. _____ study more or you will get a low grade in this course.

9. _____ be more polite. The boss doesn't like people who are rude.

10. _____ in the bathroom. She said she wanted to take a shower.

6-12 The Writing Page

A. Think about yourself. What can you do now that you couldn't do five years ago? Are there things you could do then that you can't do now? Write eight sentences comparing your abilities.

Example: I couldn't speak English five years ago, but now I can. I could climb trees easily five years ago, but now I can't.

_____

_____

_____

_____

_____

_____

_____

B. Your best friend is coming to visit your city or town for a weekend. Write a paragraph giving suggestions for things your friend can see and do. Include modals of ability, advice, possibility.

Example: You should visit the aquarium. You can't miss our great art museum.

_____

_____

_____

_____

_____

_____

_____

C. Share your paragraph from Exercise B with the class. Who has the best ideas for out-of-town visitors?

■ 6-13 Description of the Photograph

Look at the photograph below. Use it to complete the activities.

A. These two men may have a problem. They are in a religious place, and they are lighting candles, maybe to ask for help. In your notebook, use modals to write a paragraph telling what they might want help with.

B. If you really wanted or needed something in life, what would you do? For example, suppose your best friend was very sick or your car broke down and you had no money. Who could you ask for help? What actions would you take? Discuss your thoughts with a partner. Use as many modals as you can.

■ 6-14 Unit Review

Directed Writing

Task: Write a three-paragraph essay describing an unsolved or unexplained mystery.

Prewriting

Did Atlantis actually exist? Are UFOs (unidentified flying objects) real? Is there a monster in Loch Ness in Scotland? What is the meaning or purpose of the circle of stones at Stonehenge in England, or the statues on Easter Island? Choose an unsolved mystery. What are your thoughts about it? What explanations for it are possible? Do you have ideas for solving this mystery? In your notebook, make notes about the mystery you choose. Use a chart like the one below.

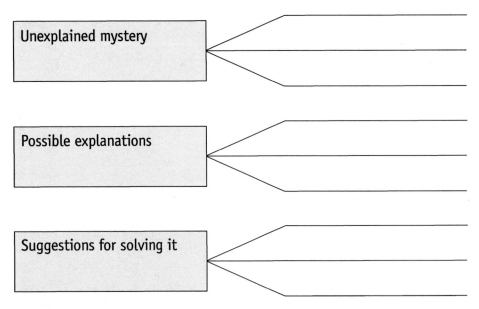

First Draft

Write a first draft of your essay. Use your chart and notes to organize your ideas as you write. Check that the first sentence of each paragraph states the main idea of the paragraph. Include what the mystery is in your first paragraph. In the second paragraph, use modals of possibility and probability to discuss explanations of the place or event. In the third paragraph, use modals of advice and ability to describe ways to study and/or solve the mystery. Remember to indent the first line in each paragraph of your essay.

> **Model** On Easter Island, there is a row of huge statues. Some of the statues are over 800 meters high. They stare out across the Pacific Ocean. Who could have built them? Why did they put the statues there?
>
> Some researchers say that people from Polynesia must have made these huge statues. They may represent some gods in their religion. The statues might be looking back to the islands in the middle of the Pacific...
>
> To solve these questions, researchers should check more stories from the different island groups in the Pacific. They ought to compare art from the islands.

Revision

Read through your essay and check for correct usage of the modals for ability, possibility, advice, and probability. Check for clear main ideas and details, and correct spelling and punctuation. Share your essay with a partner. Your partner should be able to answer the following questions about your essay:

- What is the unsolved mystery or event?
- What are some possible explanations?
- What should be done to further solve this mystery?
- Did you use modals correctly for ability, possibility, probability, and advice?
- Do you have any errors in spelling or punctuation?
- Does the essay need any more information?

Final Draft

Make any changes or additions that are needed in your essay. Then write or type a final copy. You may want to include your final essay in a portfolio of your writing.

Evaluation

Your teacher will grade your essay. You will be evaluated on:

- clarity of main ideas and level of supporting detail in your essay;
- correct usage of modals referring to present and past; and
- appropriate modals for ability, possibility, advice, and probability.

Unit 7

Imperatives and Modals of Necessity, Obligation, and Prohibition

Imperatives and modals are special verb forms. Imperatives are used for commands, and modals add particular meaning to the sentence. They are both very common forms.

Using Imperatives

Imperatives are used in the following situations:

1. **to give commands**
   Go to bed right now!   **Don't follow** me.   **Wake up.** We're late.

2. **to give instructions**
   Add two cups of sugar and **stir** well.   **Don't give** the puppy food from the table.

3. **to warn about danger**
   Look out! You almost hit me with your bag.
   Be careful. The oil in the pan is very hot.
   Don't drink that! It's paint remover, not water.

4. **to make direct requests**
   Open the door, please.   Please **lend** me a quarter.   **Don't talk** during the movie, please.
   Please makes the imperative more polite. Use it at the beginning or end of the request.

5. **to give advice**
   Eat fruit every day.   **Exercise** more often.   **Don't watch** television all the time.

Forming the Imperative

The imperative has only one form for both plural and singular subjects. Use the base form of the verb no matter how many people you are addressing.
Teacher to class: **Read** page 120.
Teacher to student: **Write** a sentence on the board.

Do not use the word *you*. It is implied, but never stated or written.
~~You~~ **Do** the dishes.   ~~You~~ **Don't take** the car.
Form the negative with *do not (don't)* + the base form of the verb.
Do not enter.   **Don't drive** drunk.

Commands with Let's and Let's not

We use *Let's* (Let us) and *Let's not* with commands to extend an invitation or make a suggestion. Unlike other commands, the speaker is included in the action.
Let's go out dancing tonight.   **Let's not work** all weekend, OK?   **Let's see** how many jelly beans there are in the bag.

Using Modals of Necessity and Obligation: *have to, must, have got to*

A. *Have to* and *must* carry the idea of necessity and obligation. *Have to* is more common than *must*. It expresses expectation. *Must* for necessity is used only in very strong or formal situations. *Have got to* implies a sense of urgency, and is most often used in spoken English.

1. with laws and rules

Tom **must take** his passport when he goes to Poland.

In the game of Monopoly, you **have to own** four houses before you can buy a hotel.

You**'ve got to take** Driver's Education before you apply for your Driver's License.

2. with strongly held cultural or family customs

I **have to go** to Thanksgiving dinner at my sister's. She cooks every year.

She **must have** a big wedding. Her mother wants it.

We **have got to call** Granny. It's her birthday.

B. *Must not* expresses a very strong prohibition, usually by an outside force.

You **must not park** there. You'll block the fire hydrant.

He **must not quit** school, or he won't get a good job.

They **must not bring** their cat. My dogs will go crazy.

C. *Don't have to* expresses freedom from a necessity, or a lack of obligation or expectation.

I **don't have to** cook tonight. My brother is taking me out to eat.

Simon **didn't have to search for a parking space** all last semester. He had a special permit for the faculty lot.

They **won't have to work** over the summer. Their parents will pay their bills.

Have got to in Oral English

Have got to is sometimes used orally to express a time or emotional crisis:

Cal **has got to stop** yelling at Yolanda. She can't live with his bad temper.

We**'ve got to arrive** at the church on time. We can't be late for the wedding.

When there is no time or emotional crisis, use *have to* or *must*:

I **have to write** a paper for my psychology class.

You **must participate** in class to get an A.

Reduced Forms of Modals

The modal *have to* is often reduced in conversation.

In informal speech, *have* and *to* are not always pronounced distinctly and sometimes end up being blended together. For example:

have to [hæftə]
has to [hæstə]
had to [hædə]

This often happens with *got* and *to* as well. They blend together into [gɑtə].

■ 7-1 Pronunciation

Read the questions in Column A. How would you respond? Write the letter of the correct response from Column B. Then practice saying the questions and answers aloud with a partner.

Column A	Column B
__D__ 1. Do we need to stop at the store?	A. Yes, we've [gɑtə] eat it. My grandmother made it.
_____ 2. Does Paul [hæftə] sing all the time?	B. I've [gɑtə] go to class.
_____ 3. Did you take the dog for a walk?	C. They [hæftə] talk to the teacher.
_____ 4. Must you play the radio so loud?	D. No, we don't [hæftə] stop, unless you need something.
_____ 5. Where's Milena?	E. I [hæftə] have it loud if I want to hear the music.
_____ 6. Why do they [hæftə] stay after class?	F. No, but he likes to.
_____ 7. Where are you going?	G. In the library. She [hæstə] study.
_____ 8. Do we [hæftə] eat that?	H. Yeah, I [hædtə] walk her, and it was raining!

◼ 7-2 Sentence Writing

Imperatives

Write three imperatives for each situation. Write at least one negative.

A. Your little brother doesn't want to go to sleep on a school night. What do you say to him?
Example: Go to your room. Don't watch television.

1. _____

2. _____

3. _____

B. You are tired, but your friend will not leave your apartment. What do you tell her?

4. _____

5. _____

6. _____

Commands with *Let's*

C. Imagine you are planning a friend's graduation party. Use commands with *Let's* to make suggestions about the party. Write at least one negative suggestion.
Example: Let's have chocolate cake. Let's not invite too many people.

7. _____

8. _____

9. _____

Modals of Necessity, Obligation, and Prohibition

D. Write about three things you have to do for school this week. Use modals of necessity or obligation.
Example: I have to go to the language lab on Tuesday.

10. _____

11. _____

12. _____

E. Write about three things that students are not allowed to do at your school. Use modals of prohibition.
Example: Students must not use cell phones in class.

13. _____

14. _____

15. _____

Look at the illustration below. Use it to complete the activities.

A. Work with a partner. Look at the picture from 1970. What do you think the mother was saying to the daughter? Use imperatives to write five sentences on the lines below. Write both affirmative and negative commands.
Example: Look at me when I speak to you! Don't take cookies.

1. _____

2. _____

3. _____

4. _____

5. _____

B. Now look at the picture from 2015. What will the daughter say to the mother? Use imperatives to write five sentences on the lines below. Will these sentences be more or less polite than in Exercise A? Why do you think so?
Example: Please be careful with your tea. Let's not break these pretty teacups.

6. _____

7. _____

8. _____

9. _____

10. _____

7-4 Communicative Activity

A. Work with a partner to fill in the table below. First, read each imperative sentence. Next, think of a place where someone might say it. Write that place in the table. Finally, think of the person who might say it in that place. Write the speaker in the table. The first one is done for you.

	Place	Speaker
Check the oil, please.	*garage*	*customer in a car*
Give me an iced tea, a double bacon cheeseburger, and fries.		
Keep your eyes on your own paper. Do not cheat!		
Pass the salt, please. You look really fantastic tonight.		
Make a list of everything you want for Christmas.		
Get out of the fast lane! You are only driving 35.		
Run around the field four times. Then take a break.		
Give me a dozen red roses, please. My girlfriend is really mad at me.		
Cash this check, please. Give me twenties and fifties.		
Let's get out of here!		

B. Now choose one of the sentences from Exercise A. Use it to begin a dialogue with your partner. Imagine you are the speaker. What else would you say? How will your partner answer? Try to talk for one minute each.

▪ 7-5 Theme-based Discussion

Read each topic below. Make sure you understand the questions. Work in groups of four to discuss the first topic. Then choose one person to report the group's answers to the class. Next move to another group to discuss the next topic. Repeat this process until all the topics are discussed.

A. Parents usually want their children to succeed. So parents often tell their children all the things they must do: go to a good college, get an important job, marry someone of their nationality. Have your parents told you that you must do certain things? Share them with your group. Do you think that you must do those things, too, or are they less important to you than to your parents? Why?

B. Think of your favorite meal. Describe it to your group and explain why it's your favorite. Use imperatives to tell your group how to make it. Give detailed instructions. When each person is finished, the group will vote on whether the meal is easy or difficult to make.

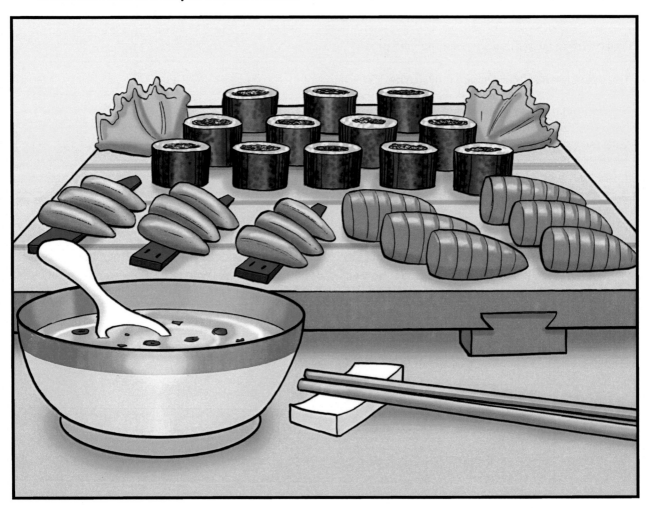

C. You are very upset. You just learned that your apartment building burned down. You have to find a new place to live as soon as possible. Take turns in your group suggesting how to find a new place. Make sure everyone speaks at least twice. Have one student write down each suggestion to share with the class.

■ 7-6 Communicative Activity: What's My Line?

A. Read through the list of occupations. Do you know what these people do at their jobs? If you're not sure, ask a classmate.

fire fighter	ski instructor
astronaut	journalist
ballet dancer	photographer
musician	marine biologist
doctor	pharmacist
zookeeper	actor/actress
pilot	artist
taxi driver	opera singer
salesperson	

B. Choose two occupations. Do not name them. Describe their requirements and duties to your partner. Use modals of necessity, obligation, and/or prohibition. Let your partner ask questions. Can your partner guess what the occupations are?

Example:

You: In my occupation, I have to wear a uniform. It's a dangerous job; I must not be careless or distracted.

Partner: Are you a police officer?

You: No, I'm not. Sometimes I've got to break walls or doors. I carry a hatchet. I must be ready to rescue people from burning buildings.

Partner: Are you a fire fighter?

You: That's right.

C. Next, your partner will choose two occupations and describe their requirements and duties to you. Your partner must also use modals of necessity, obligation, and/or prohibition. Can you guess your partner's jobs?

■ 7-7 Grammar Practice

A. You are staying in your friend's apartment while he is on vacation. He has left you a list of things to do, but some of the words are missing. Write an affirmative or negative imperative that makes sense in each blank below.

_____*Water*_____ the plants.

_____ the mail.

_____ the cat.

_____ the door.

_____ the television.

_____ the bathroom.

_____ the bills.

_____ the computer.

_____ the laundry.

_____ the car.

_____ notes for me in class.

_____ the groceries.

B. Now share your list from Exercise A with a partner. Did your partner write the same imperatives you did?

Imperatives and Modals of Necessity, Obligation, and Prohibition

■ 7-8 Error Correction

Read the sentences below. There is at least one mistake in each sentence. The mistakes could be in modal choice or form, imperative form, or extra subjects. Underline all the mistakes in each sentence, then write the sentence correctly.

1. I <u>must to read</u> in English every day.

    I must read in English every day.

2. You don't run across the street, please.

    _____

3. Mr. Grossman don't have to lecture this week.

    _____

4. Finish you the project tonight.

    _____

5. She had got to win the game.

    _____

6. Do not to let the dog out.

    _____

7. Kelley didn't had to work last summer.

    _____

8. Drank your milk!

    _____

9. Raj got to call his mother.

    _____

10. Let's us have pie for dessert.

    _____

◼ 7-9 The Writing Page

How To Do It

A. Think of a common activity, such as riding a bicycle, sending an e-mail, driving a car, using an ATM, or packing for a trip. Can you give directions clearly so another student can do the same activity? Write at least eight directions below. Use affirmative and negative imperatives.

Example: To drive a car, you must have your license and the key. First get in the car. Don't forget to put on your seat belt. Put the key in the ignition...

_____

_____

_____

_____

_____

_____

_____

_____

_____

B. Exchange directions with a partner. Read your partner's directions. Do you understand what to do? Is there anything missing? Talk about the directions and make corrections together, if needed.

Imperatives and Modals of Necessity, Obligation, and Prohibition

■ 7-10 Cloze

A. Read the story. In each blank, write a modal or imperative form from the list below. Decide if the modal should be affirmative or negative. You may use the words more than once.

have to	must	didn't have to	open	have
has to	had to	let's	stay	touch

In Greek mythology, Zeus was the most important god. The world was perfect in the beginning.

There was no sickness, no hunger, and no sorrow. There were no problems at all.

But Zeus was not happy when man learned how to use fire. He called the other gods. "We (1) ___*have to*___

do something. We (2) _____ punish man for using fire. (3) _____ create a woman. She

(4) _____ be beautiful so man will not be suspicious."

So the gods created Pandora and sent her to Earth. Epimethus saw this beautiful woman and thought,

"This (6) _____ be my lucky day!" He walked over to her and said, "(7) _____ go for a

walk." Pandora and Epimethus were happy. They (8) _____ work much.

One day, Mercury arrived carrying a beautiful box. "I (9) _____ put this heavy box down. Can I

leave it here?" Pandora said, "Of course, but you (10) _____ stay for dinner." Mercury declined, and

said that he'd be back soon. Then he added, "(11) _____ that box." Pandora and Epimethus agreed.

Pandora was curious about the beautiful box. But Epimethus reminded her, "(12) _____ away

from the box. Pandora kept looking at the box. She heard voices inside the box. "(13) _____ the

box. Let us out."

So she opened it just enough to peek inside. A swarm of hideous, winged creatures flew out. Evil, sickness,

and serious problems had escaped into the world. But then she heard one more voice coming from inside the

box. Pandora opened the box and found Hope inside. So to this day, even though there are serious problems

all over the world, people (14) _____ hold on to hope.

7-11 Imperatives

Read the imperatives below. Write a sentence explaining each imperative.

1. Don't touch that. _It's still hot._____

2. Go home. _____

3. Eat your vegetables. _____

4. Don't leave without me. _____

5. Finish your project this week. _____

6. Turn off the television. _____

7. Bring back some popcorn. _____

8. Don't drive so fast. _____

9. Fix the window. _____

10. Read your novel. _____

7-12 Sentence Conclusions

Use the sentence conclusions below to write statements about rules and laws. Use modals of necessity, prohibition and obligation. Write affirmative and negative statements.

1. _____ _We must_ _____ pay taxes every year.

2. _____ read the newspaper.

3. _____ be on time for class.

4. _____ work on Thursday.

5. _____ study until 10:00 p.m.

6. _____ know how to use a computer.

7. _____ smoke in the house.

8. _____ clean the windows in the spring.

9. _____ go to school in the summer.

10. _____ own a car.

7-13 Description of the Photograph

Look at the photograph below. Use it to complete the activities.

A. Work in pairs. Together, make a list of five imperatives that a coach or trainer might say to this athlete. Write at least one negative imperative.
Example: Run 20 laps around the track.

_____

_____

_____

_____

_____

B. With your partner, write five questions in your notebook that an interviewer might ask this athlete about training for this sport.
Example: How many hours a day do you have to practice? Do you have to eat special meals?

C. Exchange questions with another pair. For each item in Exercise B, write the athlete's response using a modal of necessity or prohibition.
Example: I have to practice four hours each day. I must not skip a day of practice.

Directed Writing

Task: Write a three-paragraph essay presenting your ideas for solving a problem.

Prewriting

Our world today has many problems: war, pollution, hunger, disease, crime. However, we hope that people will work together to solve these problems. Choose a specific problem. Now, what are your ideas for solving it? What do people have to do? What must happen for the situation to change? In your notebook, make notes about the problem you chose. Use a chart like the one below:

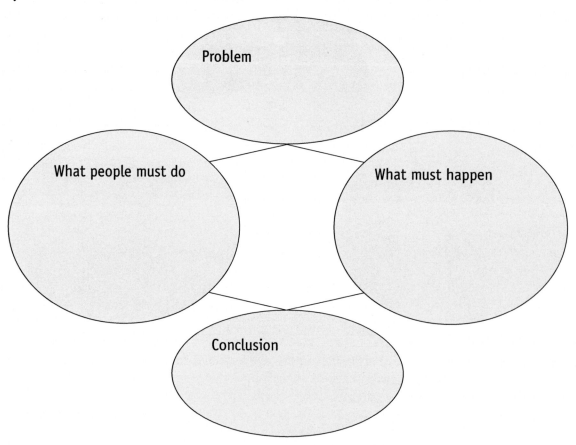

First Draft

Write a first draft of your essay. Use your chart and notes to organize your ideas as you write. Check that the first sentence of each paragraph states the main idea of the paragraph. Use modals of necessity, obligation, and prohibition to discuss necessary actions to solve the problem. Use commands with *Let's* and *Let's not* to make suggestions. Remember to indent the first line in each paragraph of your essay.

Model
> The oceans are becoming polluted. This is a major problem. Pollution kills fish, animals, and plants. We must do something to prevent more pollution.
>
> Fish are a major food source. They must have a clean environment to live. We have to stop...
>
> Ocean plants are a food source for the fish and also one of the largest sources of oxygen. We must protect...
>
> Everyone needs the ocean. Let's keep the oceans clean. We all must take part in caring for it. We have to control...

Revision

Read through your essay and check for correct usage of commands with *Let's* and the modals for prohibition, obligation, and necessity. Check that your main idea is clear and that you have supporting details. Correct spelling and punctuation. Share your essay with a partner. Your partner should be able to answer the following questions about your essay:

- What problem are you discussing?
- What must people do to solve the problem?
- What must be prohibited?
- Did you use modals correctly?
- Did you use commands with *Let's* correctly?
- Do you have any errors in spelling or punctuation?
- Does the essay need any more information?

Final Draft

Make any changes or additions that are needed in your essay. Then write or type a final copy. You may want to include your final essay in a portfolio of your writing.

Evaluation

Your teacher will grade your essay. You will be evaluated on:

- clarity of main ideas and good supporting details in your essay;
- correct use of affiirmative and negative imperatives and commands with *Let's*; and
- correct use and variety of modals of necessity, obligation and prohibition.

Unit 8

The Noun Phrase

Think of grammar as a number of building blocks. First, there are single units called **words**. Next, there are larger units made up of groups of words. These larger units can be **phrases, clauses,** or **sentences**. This unit focuses on one type of phrase, **the noun phrase**. In order to understand noun phrases thoroughly, it is important to know how they are different from other phrases as well as from clauses and sentences.

1. **Phrases**

   Phrases are groups of words that *do not* contain a subject and verb. Noun phrases contain nouns, adjectives, and determiners (numbers, articles, demonstrative or possessive adjectives, or quantifiers).
   That big brown cow
   Cinderella's two ugly stepsisters

2. **Clauses**

   Clauses are groups of words that contain a subject and verb; however, clauses aren't always complete thoughts.
   When **he gets** out of jail
   As long as **I love** him

3. **Sentences**

   Sentences are groups of words that contain *both* a subject and verb and express a complete thought.
   Heidi doesn't want to go to the movies.
   Have you seen the new car?

Noun Phrase Positions Within a Sentence

As you can see from the examples above, a noun phrase contains a noun and the determiners or adjectives that describe it. The noun phrase may be in the **subject** or the **object/complement** position in a sentence. If it is in the object/complement position, then the noun phrase may be the object of a verb or the object of a preposition.

Noun Phrases in the Subject Position
My ring finger is large.
Our gorgeous oval antique white Chinese porcelain serving platter is lost.

Noun Phrases in the Object/Complement Position
Louis is **a sweet, small, young, black and tan English Setter.**
I have been thinking about **a hot buttered blueberry muffin** all morning.

Positions Within a Noun Phrase

There are three positions within a noun phrase:

Position #1	Position #2	Position #3
Determiners	Descriptive Adjectives	The Noun

Position #1 is for determiners. Determiners can be numbers, articles, demonstrative or possessive adjectives, or quantifiers.

Demonstrative Adjective Possessive Adjective Article	Quantifier Number	Noun
Those	few	cats
My	two	dollars
The	six	children
An		apple

Position #2 is for descriptive adjectives that tell *what kind* of noun:

My **ring** finger

The **gorgeous oval antique white Chinese porcelain serving** platter

That **sweet small young black and tan** English Setter

Position #3 is for the noun. The noun is the last word in the noun phrase. Remember that the noun can be singular or plural, count or noncount, common or proper, concrete or abstract.

Adjective Order in Noun Phrases

If there is more than one adjective in a noun phrase, the adjectives usually follow a pattern based on the characteristic they describe.

Your opinion of the noun	size	shape	age	color	origin	material	special use	noun
beautiful	big	round	new	red	Polish	wooden	mixing	bowl
delicate	small	square	old	blue	Peruvian	porcelain	cocoa	pot

Most noun phrases have only some of these descriptive adjectives. If a particular adjective is missing, its placement is ignored.

Pronouns in Follow-up Sentences

If a follow-up sentence refers to the noun, a pronoun is used to replace the noun or noun phrase:

NOUN PHRASE	**VERB PHRASE**	**PREPOSITIONAL PHRASE**
Cinderella's two ugly stepsisters	bought dresses	for themselves.

PRONOUN	**PRONOUN**	**PRONOUN**
Theirs were ugly, so	*they* were perfect for	*them.*

Look at the arrows. Note that the form of each pronoun in the follow-up sentence depends on its function in the sentence: is it the subject, the object, or does it express possession?

Use commas to separate two or more equal adjectives that describe the same noun. Do not add an extra comma between the final adjective and the noun itself. Also do not use commas if one adjective is not equal to another.

Two adjectives in a row are equal if:
the sentence makes sense if the adjectives are written in reverse order.
OR
the sentence makes sense if *and* is written between the adjectives.

Equal Adjectives
He was a **difficult, stubborn** child.   (He was a difficult and stubborn child.)
The **hot, powerful** sun burned my nose.   (The hot and powerful sun burned my nose.)

Unequal Adjectives
They lived in a **red brick** building.
We often wore a **gray wool** scarf and hat.
The **hot summer** sun beat down on them.

8-1 Commas and Adjective Order in Noun Phrases

Read each noun phrase below. Arrange the words in the correct order and write the phrase on the line. Add commas where needed. When you are finished, practice saying each phrase with a partner.

1. office huge downtown beautiful new   *beautiful, huge, new downtown office*

2. sweater green her and striped white _____

3. old cramped apartment dirty their _____

4. strong gorgeous tall trees leafy three _____

5. story fascinating long a mystery _____

6. orange skinny cat young shy _____

7. large class rowdy unpredictable loud _____

8. phones modern sleek several compact expensive _____

■ 8-2 Noun Phrase Writing

Imagine that you are hungry and thirsty. You are in a huge supermarket, and you can pick out anything you want, from any country. As you walk through the aisles, your mouth begins to water. In the exercises below, describe what you would like to eat or drink. As you compose your noun phrases, make sure to use many different determiners and descriptive adjectives.

A. Think of four noun phrases describing what you want to pick out first. Put them in sentences that begin with: *I want _____ .*

Example: I want that beautiful, round, rosy Gala apple. I want the biggest candy bar in the store.

1. _____

2. _____

3. _____

4. _____

B. Now look only at vegetables. Think of four noun phrases that will make anyone want to eat them. Put them in sentences that begin with: *You will love _____ .*

Example: You will love those fresh, long green beans. You will love a few large, red Bermuda onions.

5. _____

6. _____

7. _____

8. _____

C. You are now in the bakery section of the supermarket. What will you get for dinner or dessert? Think of four noun phrases that describe what you would like. Put them in the following sentence: *I will get _____ for dinner/dessert.*

Example: I will get some small Southern biscuits for dinner. I will get several chocolate nut brownies for dessert.

9. _____

10. _____

11. _____

12. _____

Look at the illustration. Use it to complete the activities.

A. Talk about the illustration with a group. Which feature do you like most? A feature is a specific detail, such as a person, an animal, or a thing in an illustration, or it might be the overall composition. It also could be the way the lines are drawn, the color, or shading, or the humor or seriousness of the subject.

B. Ask a class recorder to list on the board all the features that the class thought were the most interesting. Then vote as a class and eliminate all but the two most popular features on the list.

C. Choose two class debaters: one to speak for one feature in the illustration and the other to speak for the other feature. After the debate, vote again and see which feature the majority of people in your class likes the most.

■ 8-4 Theme-based Discussion

Read each topic below. Make sure you understand the questions. Work in groups of four to discuss the first topic. Then choose one person to report the group's answers to the class. Next move to another group to discuss the next topic. Repeat this process until all the topics are discussed. Spend the first 20 minutes defining what social class means with the class. Ask someone to be the class recorder and write your ideas on the board.

A. With your group, explore these questions: What does *social class* mean? What class were you born into? Most Americans will say that they were born into the middle class, but what does that really mean? Are most societies divided into a lower class, a middle class, and an upper class?

B. In the United States, there are many idioms that are related in some way to social class. Read the sentences below and pay attention to the class-based idioms. What do you think they mean? Which ones are associated with the upper class? Which with the lower class? Discuss their meanings as your recorder takes notes to share with the class.

Class-based Idioms:

He was born **with a silver spoon in his mouth.**   She is a real **social climber.**
She is **an uptown girl.**   He is a **name-dropper.**
They were born **on the wrong side of the tracks.**   He's a **blue-collar worker.**

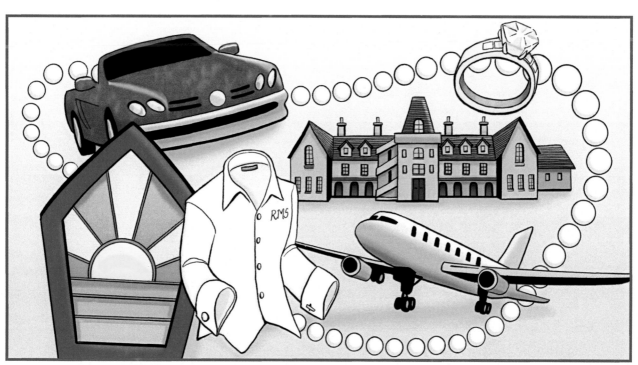

C. In stories and biographies, very often a writer will define someone's class by naming certain things that a person has or is exposed to. Read the list of those things below. Which class is associated with each item? Why do you think so?

stained glass windowpanes	**monogrammed shirts**	**older cars**
minivans	**cognac**	**beer**
	white picket fence	

D. In your notebook, list three things that are associated with the upper class, middle class, and lower class in your native country. Explain to your group why each item is associated with that class.

A. Read the story of Jack the Giant Killer. Underline all the nouns or noun phrases in the passage.

Jack the Giant Killer

When King Arthur reigned, there lived in the county of Cornwall a farmer who had a son named Jack. He was very smart with a quick wit. No one could defeat him.

In those days, Mount Cornwall was guarded by a huge giant named Cormoran. He was eighteen feet tall and about nine feet around. He had a fierce, grim face and was the terror of all the nearby towns and villages. He lived in a cave in the rugged mountain. Whenever he wanted food, he would wade over to the mainland where he would take for himself whatever he wanted. When people saw him, they ran out of their houses. He took their cattle and carried a dozen oxen on his back at a time. He tied the sheep and hogs around his waist. He had done this for so many years that all of Cornwall despaired.

One day, Jack was in the town hall when the members of the town council were discussing the giant. The poor young lad asked: "What reward will be given to the man who kills Cormoran?"

"The giant's treasure will be the reward," they said.

"Then I'll do it," said Jack.

Jack got a horn, shovel, and an axe. He went to Mount Cornwall just as it started to get dark. Before morning, he had dug a pit 22 feet deep and nearly as wide, and covered it with long sticks and straw. Then he spread a little mold over the sticks and straw so that it looked like plain ground. Jack then sat on the opposite side of the pit, farthest away from the giant's cave. At sunrise, he put the horn to his mouth and blew, *Tantivy, Tantivy*. This noise woke up the giant, who rushed from his cave crying: "You horrible man, you have disturbed my rest! You shall pay dearly for this. I will take you whole and broil you for breakfast!" But just as he finished speaking, the giant tumbled into the pit. The mountain shook when he fell. "Oh, Giant," said Jack, "where are you now? Oh, look, you've fallen into Lob's Pound. What do you think now of broiling me for your breakfast? Will no other diet serve you but poor Jack?" After Jack teased the giant for a while, he hit the giant on the head with his axe, and killed him on the spot.

Jack then filled up the pit with earth and went to search the giant's cave. He found a fortune in treasure. When the council heard of the giant's death, they presented Jack with a sword and a belt. They were embroidered in gold with these words:

"Here's the brave Cornish man who slew the giant Cormoran."

The council declared that from that day forward, he would be known as Jack the Giant Killer.

B. Read the story again with a partner. Make sure you have found all the nouns or noun phrases. On the lines below, write each noun or noun phrase and indicate its function (Subject, Object of a Verb, Object of a Preposition).

_____	_____	_____
_____	_____	_____
_____	_____	_____
_____	_____	_____
_____	_____	_____
_____	_____	_____
_____	_____	_____
_____	_____	_____

■ 8-6 Creative Listings

A. Make a list of four people you remember from elementary school. Write two sentences about each of them, using noun phrases. In the first sentence, use a descriptive phrase. In the second sentence, tell what they are doing now. If you are not sure, guess.

Example: Name: *Henry Rodriguez*

Henry was a good student. Henry is now a boring accountant.

_____

_____

_____

_____

_____

_____

_____

B. Now make a list of the four best gifts that you have ever given or received. Write a sentence about each gift, using a noun phrase to describe it.

Example: Gift: *ring*

I gave a beautiful diamond ring to my fiancé.

_____

_____

_____

_____

C. Finally, make a list of four different jobs. Then write a sentence about a good characteristic associated with each job, using a noun phrase.

Example: Job: *teacher*

A good teacher is very patient.

_____

_____

_____

_____

■ 8-7 Grammar in Action

"In-Your-Face" Idioms

The face and its various parts are involved in many noun phrases, which are also idioms.

A. Read the **In-Your-Face Idioms** box. See if you can guess the meanings of the idioms from context clues in the example sentences.

to be/get in (one's) face	The coach **got in my face** and screamed at me.
to be (very) cheeky	She **is very cheeky** sometimes. She walked right into her boss' office and started to explain what was wrong with the company.
to turn the other cheek	You should forgive people who hurt you. You should always **turn the other cheek.**
to only have eyes for	Christie **only has eyes for** Paul. She won't dance with or talk to anyone else.
an eye for an eye	He believes in revenge. He always says **an eye for an eye** and a tooth for a tooth.
the evil eye	Helga doesn't like her neighbor. When she sees him, she always gives him **the evil eye.**
to have a big mouth	Adriano certainly **has a big mouth.** He just can't keep a secret.
to have a dirty mouth	That boy **has a dirty mouth.** He curses all the time. His mother didn't teach him to talk that way.
to put (one's) foot in (one's) mouth	Every time I visit my in-laws, I really **put my foot in my mouth.** I always say the wrong thing.
to read (one's) lips	**Read my lips.** I'm serious. I will not let you copy my homework.
to lick (one's) lips	When they found they were playing Joliet Junior College, they began **to lick their lips.** They thought they would win very easily.
to play it by ear	Let's **play it by ear.** I'm not sure if I can go to the party. Maybe I'll meet you there.
to have an ear for (something)	That child **has an ear for** music. She can play piano just by listening.
to be all ears	I really want to hear your story. I **am all ears.**
to have a nose for	My mother **has a nose for** bargains. She can find great sales everywhere.
to be (way) over (one's) head	I can't do this trigonometry problem. It **is way over my head.**

B. Share your guesses with the class. Were you able to figure out the meaning?

C. Take turns asking and answering the following questions with a partner. Write your partner's answers in your notebook.

Do you know someone with a big mouth? Who?
When are you "all ears"?

Do you like to play your weekends by ear, or do you like to plan them? Why?
Have you ever put your foot in your mouth? What happened?
Is your philosophy "to turn the other cheek" or "an eye for an eye"? Why?

■ 8-8 Error Correction

Read the sentences below. Each sentence has at least one mistake. The mistakes could be in determiners, order, or form of descriptive adjectives. Underline all the mistakes in each sentence, then write the sentence correctly.

1. <u>The</u> my cat loves to sleep <u>on couch</u>.

   My cat loves to sleep on the couch.

2. This the book on the table is Henry's.

   _____

3. Her reds shoes are perfect for dancing.

   _____

4. My brother tall is a really good cook. He is always in kitchen.

   _____

5. Hilda kissed the her boyfriend on cheek.

   _____

6. Three man bought a car expensive from a dealer dishonest.

   _____

7. Several hungry man ate him sandwich in one minutes.

   _____

8. The Professor Morandi is patient person.

   _____

9. My sister met the her boyfriend on bus going to the Philadelphia.

   _____

10. My the favorite book is *Love in the Time of Cholera*.

    _____

11. She's house red is located near a hazardous waste dump, but she loves it.

    _____

12. In summer, the boy always looks at girl on beach.

    _____

13. The photograph black and white at end of chapter is interesting.

    _____

■ 8-9 Sentence Stems

Use the sentence stems below to write statements using noun phrases as both subjects and objects. Write affirmative and negative statements. Make sure to use determiners and descriptive adjectives.

1. After the war, *my older brother came home from the Army.* _____

2. My lazy cousin _____

3. Those beautiful roses _____

4. Cristiana received this expensive _____

5. The elegant movie star _____

6. The clever thief stole _____

7. Many intelligent people _____

8. The tall man drank strong _____

9. Your beautiful new car _____

10. That man on the bench _____

■ 8-10 Sentence Conclusions

Use the sentence conclusions below to write statements using noun phrases as both subjects and objects. Write affirmative and negative statements. Make sure to use determiners and descriptive adjectives.

1. _____ hiding under the bed.

2. _____ with a gigantic nose.

3. _____ from her boyfriend.

4. _____ a beautiful black dress.

5. _____ in a dark and secret place.

6. _____ about their very first date.

7. _____ for my 21st birthday.

8. _____ until the end of time.

9. _____ at 4:32 a.m. on Saturday.

10. _____ a new couch and love seat.

8-11 The Writing Page

Below is a list of noun phrase-subjects, verbs, and noun phrase-objects/complements. Combine these elements in as many ways as you can to make 10 logical (if silly) sentences. Write both affirmative and negative sentences in any tense. When you are finished, share your sentences with a group. Did you choose the same verbs and objects to go with each subject? Why do you think so?

Subjects	Verbs	Objects/Complements
This purple flower	be	a lily/lilies
That pale bride	make	over $100
My 52 CDs	have	a lot of money
His really bad painting	like	a great smelling perfume
Valentine's Day	follow	a miracle/miracles
My brother	cost	bets in his/her spare time
That cookbook	do	very bushy eyebrows
The man nearest me	want	some medicine
The woman farthest from me	buy	tender care
Our teacher	hit	very young women
His smile	need	many men and women
An apple pie	guide	all of Elvis's songs
Albert Einstein's ideas	offend	a great deal of knowledge
Tart green apples	contain	a rest
Some houses	create	many enemies
Pets	inspire	a new computer
		oxygen
		many possibilities
		New Year's Day

1. _____

2. _____

3. _____

4. _____

5. _____

6. _____

7. _____

8. _____

9. _____

10. _____

8-12 Description of the Photograph

Look at the photograph. Use it to complete the activities.

A. Work with a partner. Talk about what is happening in the photograph. Write a story on the lines below using noun phrases.

_____

_____

_____

_____

_____

_____

_____

_____

_____

B. In the photograph, a storm is rapidly approaching. Were you ever caught in a storm? Or have you ever watched a terrible storm from your window? Tell the story in your notebook. Use noun phrases to describe what happened.

■ 8-13 Unit Review

Directed Writing

Task: Write a three-paragraph essay about an interesting fictional character.

Prewriting

Who do you think is the most interesting character in a movie or book? Superman? Lady Macbeth? Don Quixote? Ace Ventura? Alice in Wonderland? What is this character like? What do other characters think or say about him or her? What makes this character is so interesting? In your notebook, make notes about your choice for the most interesting character. Use a chart like the one below.

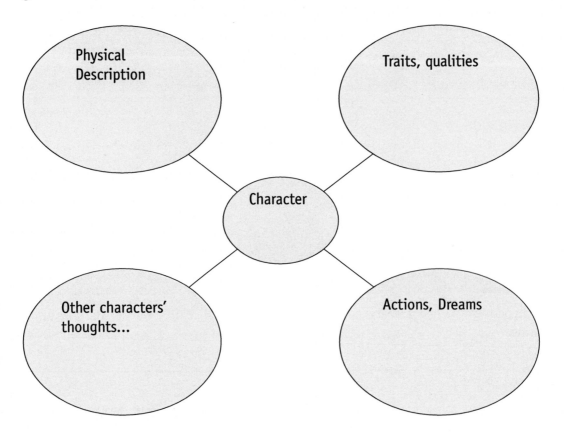

First Draft

Write a first draft of your essay. Use your chart and notes to organize your ideas as you write. Check that your first paragraph describes your favorite character. Use the second paragraph to explain how other characters feel about your chosen character. Make sure that your third paragraph concludes the essay, stating why you think this is the most interesting character. Use noun phrases.

> **Model**
>
> My favorite movie character is not an educated man, but he was a strong and determined person. He lived in a poor section of Philadelphia...
>
> Rocky had a trainer and coach. This old retired coach believed in Rocky and loved him. He wanted Rocky to win...
>
> Rocky worked hard to be a champion heavyweight boxer. Everything he did helped him...

Revision

Read through your essay and check for correct word order, correct usage of determiners and adjectives in noun phrases, clear main idea and details, and correct spelling and punctuation. Share your essay with a partner. Your partner should be able to answer the following questions about your essay:

- Who is your favorite character?
- What is he or she like?
- How do the other characters feel about your favorite character?
- Did you use determiners and adjectives correctly in noun phrases?
- Do you have any errors in spelling or punctuation?
- Does the essay need any more information?

Final Draft

Make any changes or additions that are needed in your essay. Then write or type a final copy. You may want to include your final essay in a portfolio of your writing.

Evaluation

Your teacher will grade your essay. You will be evaluated on:

- clarity of ideas and level of supporting detail in your essay;
- correct use and placement of determiners in noun phrases; and
- correct use and placement of adjectives in noun phrases.

Unit 9

The Passive Voice

In past units, we studied verb tense. Verb tense tells us whether the verb is referring to past, present, or future time. We also studied subject–verb agreement, which tells us whether the verb should be singular or plural. In this unit, we will study another feature of English verbs: their "voice."

Voice in English Verbs

Verbs in English are in one of three voices: **active**, **passive**, and **imperative.**

The **active voice** is used when the subject of the sentence performs the action. This is the voice used in most English sentences, in the usual pattern of subject-verb-object.

The **passive voice** is used when the subject does not perform the action but instead is the object (receiver) of it. The passive voice is not as common as the active voice. In this unit we will analyze when to use the passive voice.

The **imperative voice** is used for commands and requests. The imperative is the base form of the verb. We studied the imperative in Unit 7.

Using the Passive Voice

Generally, to emphasize the object (receiver) of an action instead of the subject (performer), use the passive voice.

Active: **The coach yelled** at my brother during the big game.

Passive: **My brother was yelled at** by the coach during the big game.

The passive voice is used in the following situations:

1. **to describe what someone or something created, built, or destroyed**
   The Ninth Symphony **was first performed** by Beethoven in 1824.
   Much of New Orleans **is still devastated.**
   The new technology center **will be completed** next summer.

2. **when you don't know or it isn't important who performed an action**
   I **have been robbed** twice in Boston.
   The news **hasn't been broadcast** yet.
   My new coat **will be hand-sewn.**

3. **in prepositional phrases with** *by*
   Her portrait **is being painted by** her son.
   The lithium-ion battery **was patented by** Dr. John Goodenough.
   The money **will be repaid by** the insurance company.

4. **in expressions with** *get*
   You **get called on** in every class.
   Morticia **got hired** as assistant director at Bedeger's Funeral Parlor.
   They **got married** in a large hall.

To form the passive voice, use a form of *be* + the past participle. Changing the form of the *be* verb changes the tense of the sentence.

Simple Present
Students **are invited** to try the delicacies at the cafeteria in East Hall.

Simple Past
He **was born** in a taxicab on the Brooklyn Bridge.

Simple Future
My best friend **will be divorced** by this time next year.

Present Perfect
Mario's cousin **has been accepted** to the medical school at the University of Pennsylvania.

Present Progressive
I promise you the problem **is being taken care of**.

Past Progressive
As they walked into the stadium, the star player **was being carried off** the field.

With the passive voice, the *by* phrase is optional.

John's bicycle **was crushed** (by a car).
The books **were knocked off** the shelf (by a student).
The research **will be done** (by Antonio).
All the paperwork **will be shredded** (by the bank employees).

The Stative Passive

A common construction in English is the combination of the verb *be* and the past participle, which then becomes an adjective.

Active or Passive Voice	Stative Passive as adjective
My sister **was married** three years ago.	Now she **is married**.
I **locked** the car before I came in the house.	Now the car **is locked**.

Active vs. Passive

The passive voice is commonly used to discuss certain situations. For example, discussions about crime often involve very active verbs, such as *killed* and *robbed*. So why is the passive voice, rather than the active voice, often used to talk about crimes?

One reason is that the criminal's identity is often unknown or uncertain. Another reason is to emphasize the victim, rather than the criminal. If we know the name of the victim, but not the criminal, it is logical to use the passive voice.

Javi's car **was stolen** last week.

When we can identify the criminal, the active voice can be used.

John Wilkes Booth **assassinated** President Lincoln in 1865.

■ 9-1 Active vs. Passive

Read each sentence below. Decide if it is active **(A)** or passive **(P)**. Write the correct letter in the blank. Rewrite each active sentence as a passive sentence, with or without a *by* phrase. Be careful to use the same tense.

1. _____*A*_____ I lost the necklace yesterday.

   The necklace was lost yesterday.

2. _____ The man was found "not guilty."

   _____

3. _____ Civil war has affected many countries.

   _____

4. _____ Rik is firing Alma this week.

   _____

5. _____ Pine Grove police officers will catch the thief.

   _____

6. _____ Fourteen people were hurt in the bus accident.

   _____

7. _____ The storm cut power to the whole town.

   _____

8. _____ The principal will give both girls a warning about their behavior.

   _____

■ 9-2 Sentence Writing

Something Created, Built or Destroyed

A. Use the passive voice to write three sentences about building construction. In each sentence, use one of these phrases: *in the 1930s, right now,* and *five hundred years from now.* Pay particular attention to the verb tenses required by these phrases.
Example: In the 1930s, very few new homes were built.

1. _____

2. _____

3. _____

B. Use the passive voice to write three sentences about art, literature, or music. Use verbs such as *composed, written,* and *performed.* You can use prepositional phrases with *by.*
Example: My favorite song was written by John Lennon in 1967.

4. _____

5. _____

6. _____

C. Use the passive voice to write two sentences about objects or products. Use verbs such as *make, manufacture, grow,* and *produce.* Use at least two different tenses. You can use prepositional phrases with *by.*
Example: Most coffee in the United States is grown in South America.

7. _____

8. _____

D. Use the passive voice to write two sentences about natural disasters. Use participles such as *destroyed, flattened, knocked down,* and *burned down.*
Example: A big part of New Orleans was destroyed by floods.

9. _____

10. _____

Get + past participle

E. Use expressions with *get* + past participle to write three sentences about your past, present, or future jobs. Use *hired* and *fired.*
Example: I got hired at my first job in 2002.

11. _____

12. _____

13. _____

Look at the illustration. Use it to complete the activities.

A. A conflagration, or large, destructive fire, has just struck the downtown area of your city. With a partner, imagine that you are newspaper reporters who are sent to write about the story. Write notes below telling what you see at the scene.

Notes

_____

_____

_____

_____

_____

B. Now use your notes to write a paragraph in your notebook describing the damage from the fire. Since no one knows who or what caused the fire, you should use the passive voice as often as possible. Write at least 10 sentences.

■ 9-4 Cloze

The passage below is about the U.S. Electoral College. With a partner, read the passage and write a passive voice verb from the box in each blank. The verbs can be in the past, present, or future tense. Use each verb only once. Remember to make the verbs and subjects agree.

add	elect	punch
argue	give	reach
award	grant	surprise
choose	need	use
contest		

How the President is Elected

In 2000, George W. Bush won the U.S. presidential election. But he didn't win the popular vote. His opponent, Al Gore, got more votes than he did. How did that happen? Since 1789, three other presidents have taken office without winning the popular vote. In order to understand how these presidents (1) _____were elected_____ , we must understand how something called the Electoral College works.

The Electoral College system (2) _____ to elect the president and vice president. The number of electoral votes each state gets (3) _____ by adding the number of its senators and representatives in Congress together. In a presidential election, the candidate who receives the highest number of popular votes in a state (4) _____ all of that state's electoral votes.

The total number of electoral votes in the country is 538. There are 435 members of the House of Representatives and 100 senators. In addition, the District of Columbia, the capital of the United States, (5) _____ three electoral votes. A candidate needs to win at least half the electoral votes to become president. So, 270 of the 538 electoral votes (6) _____ to win.

In the 2000 presidential election, the votes in the state of Florida (7) _____ still _____ one month after election day. Many Americans (8) _____ to learn that the small perforated paper ballot (9) _____ not completely _____ by many voters. The decision whether to count these irregular paper ballots or not led to a long delay in deciding who won the state's electoral votes. The case (10) _____ by lawyers in both the Florida courts and the U.S. Supreme Court. When the Supreme Court of the United States decided that these irregular ballots should not be counted, George W. Bush won that state's popular vote and (11) _____ Florida's 25 electoral votes.

When those votes (12) _____ to his total from other states, Bush had enough electoral votes to win the election.

The president (13) _____ in the same way in future elections, so a candidate who loses the popular vote could win the office again.

Read each topic below. Make sure you understand the questions. Work in groups of four to discuss the first topic. Choose one person to report the group's answers to the class. Then move to another group to discuss the next topic. Repeat this process until all the topics are discussed. Try to speak to people you haven't spoken to before.

A. Reread the cloze exercise in Activity 9–4. In groups of four, discuss how the American president is chosen. Refer to the passage and try to analyze and memorize the method. Do you think that the American system is a true democracy?

B. Now, analyze how leaders are chosen in your native country. How does the system work? Write down a few ideas in your notebook and explain them to the other members of your group. Then discuss the advantages and disadvantages of these systems.

C. News stories on television and radio and in newspapers pay a great deal of attention to natural disasters and the damage that they cause. Perhaps you remember Hurricane Katrina in the late summer of 2005. In small groups, discuss what happens when a hurricane hits an area.
(Note: Use present tense passive.)

• What happened in the particular case of Hurricane Katrina?
(Note: Use past tense passive.)

• Imagine that next summer, another terrible storm, named Hurricane Kevin, will strike the Gulf Coast. What do you think will happen?
(Note: Use the future passive.)

9-6 Grammar Practice

Look at each active sentence below. Circle the subject and draw a square around the object. Then underline the verb and analyze its tense and number. If possible, rewrite each sentence as a passive sentence. Prepositional phrases with *by* are optional. If it is not possible to rewrite the sentence in the passive voice, write "NO CHANGE."

Example:

Active sentence:

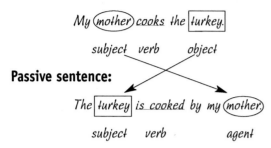

Passive sentence:

1. The Pilgrims started Thanksgiving many years ago.

   _____

2. Thanksgiving is an important holiday in the United States.

   _____

3. On Thanksgiving, New York City holds a big parade.

   _____

4. Many American families will cook turkeys.

   _____

5. I will go to my friend's house for Thanksgiving.

   _____

6. People will buy a lot of food for the holiday.

   _____

7. Students will serve meals to homeless people.

   _____

8. The president will give a talk on the radio.

   _____

9. My family held a big party last year.

   _____

10. Someone will close school for the next two days.

    _____

■ 9-7 Grammar Discussion

One of the most common phrases in English is "It's not my fault." That's what some people say when they are confronted with a mistake that they do not want to admit. For example, if you go to the bursar's office and find out that your tuition check has been lost, you would be surprised if the cashier there said, "Oh, yes. I lost your check. I just can't seem to find it!" Instead, he probably will say, "Your check has been lost." By using the passive voice, he does not have to say who is at fault. Other similar examples are:

- Your refund check has been sent. (When was it sent? When can I expect to get it?)
- Seven soldiers have been killed. (Who killed them? What exactly happened?)
- I'm sorry. Your house was destroyed by a fire. (What caused the fire?)

There are many other situations in which people might not want to admit mistakes. For each situation below, write three sentences that someone might use to avoid admitting a mistake. Use passive voice.

A. Situation: One of your roommates ate the last cookie and put the empty box back in the cupboard.

1. _____

2. _____

3. _____

B. Situation: A secret Senate memo has been given to the press.

4. _____

5. _____

6. _____

C. Situation: A rare and expensive book is missing from the library.

7. _____

8. _____

9. _____

9-8 Sentence Analysis

Present and past participles are often used as adjectives. In general, the *-ed* adjective shows that the person or thing (usually the subject) receives the action/feeling.
Example: I was surprised by the number of people.

Generally, the *-ing* adjective shows that the person or thing (usually the subject) causes the action/feeling.
Example: The movie was surprising.

A. With a partner, study the following sentences. Circle the present participles and underline the past participles. Draw a line from each participle to the noun it describes.

1. The boring movie made the entire audience yawn.

2. The amazed audience didn't move an inch during the performance.

3. Their disappointed teacher told them to stay after class.

4. The best-seller wasn't a very interesting novel.

5. That annoying little boy won't stop screaming.

6. The surprising news left everyone shocked.

7. She wanted to pet my sleeping dog.

8. Computerized translators will work better in the future.

B. With your partner, talk about the different meanings of the following pairs of participial adjectives. Write one sentence using each word to show the difference.

1. amazing/amazed

_____

_____

2. depressing/depressed

_____

_____

3. annoying/annoyed

_____

_____

4. confusing/confused

_____

_____

■ 9-9 Grammar in Action

A. Interview a partner. Use the participles below to ask questions with "Have you ever been _____?"
Write your partner's answer to each question on the lines below. Use full sentences.

married	embarrassed	robbed	lost	hurt
fired	confused			

1. _____

   _____

2. _____

   _____

3. _____

   _____

4. _____

   _____

5. _____

   _____

6. _____

   _____

7. _____

   _____

B. Now read your partner's answers from Exercise A. If they answered yes to any question, ask them "What happened when you were _____?"

9-10 Error Correction

Read the sentences below. Each sentence has at least one mistake. The mistakes could be in verb form, subject–verb agreement, or choice of active or passive voice. Underline all the mistakes in each sentence, then write the sentence correctly.

1. I got <u>boring</u> because the movie was so <u>uninterested</u>.

   I got bored because the movie was so uninteresting.

2. Many strange things were happened last night.

   _____

3. I was hurt my leg because I hit by a car.

   _____

4. In class yesterday, I was confusing because I was not understand the lesson.

   _____

5. The phonograph invented by Edison, who borned in 1847.

   _____

6. The children frightened by the dog, but the dog was not hurt anyone.

   _____

7. The bridges over the Arno River in Florence was builded in the 14th century.

   _____

8. Nick was firing from his job because he was insulted his boss.

   _____

9. I lost in the old part of the city since were not too many signs.

   _____

10. My grandfather was died in the war, about 10 years before I was borned.

    _____

11. Engineers start by construction on the Golden Gate Bridge in 1933.

    _____

12. That car designed by the first female car designer in America.

    _____

■ 9-11 Description of the Photograph

Look at the photograph. Use it to complete the activities.

A. Write eight sentences describing the man in the picture. Who is he? What important things have happened to him in his life? In each sentence, use the passive voice.

1. _____

2. _____

3. _____

4. _____

5. _____

6. _____

7. _____

8. _____

B. Now share your sentences with the class. Are your ideas the same as your classmates'? Why do you think yours are correct? Use clues in the photograph to support your ideas.

9-12 The Writing Page

Expository Writing

A. Choose a topic from the list below or use one of your own and research it on the Internet. Search engines such as yahoo.com, google.com, and ask.com are good places to start. Take notes in your notebook about the main ideas you decide to use.

Human development from birth to age 1
Airplane takeoff or landing processes
How to bake bread
World history for the year 1999
Growth of e-commerce
Evolution of stem-cell research

B. Use your notes to write an informational paragraph about your topic. Use the passive voice as much as possible.

_____

_____

_____

_____

_____

_____

_____

_____

Creative Grammar **149**

Directed Writing

Task: Write a three-paragraph essay about a discovery or invention.

Prewriting

What do you think was the most important discovery or invention in the history of the world? Thomas Edison's light bulb? Pascal's calculating machine (ancestor to the computer)? The wheel? The microscope? The discovery of DNA? The human genome program? The discovery of new solar systems?

Why do you think that invention or discovery is so important? What has happened since it was invented or discovered? What impact could this discovery or invention have on the future? In your notebook, make notes about your choice for the most important discovery or invention. Use a chart like the one below.

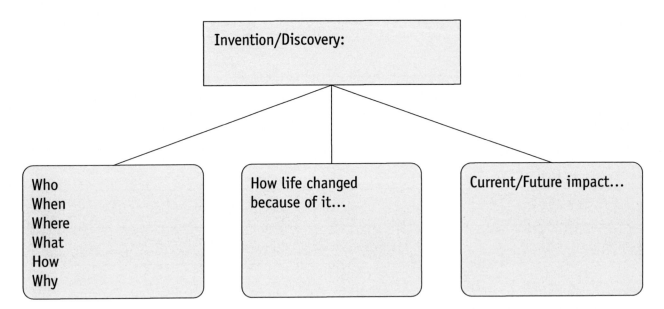

First Draft

Write a first draft of your essay. Use your chart and notes to organize your ideas as you write. Check that your first paragraph gives the basic information about this discovery or invention. Use the second paragraph to describe the impact this invention/discovery has had on the world. Make sure that your third paragraph concludes the essay, stating why you think this is the most important discovery/invention and what its future impact might be. Use the passive voice and participles as adjectives.

> **Model**
>
> Printing with moveable type had been done in Asia since the 700s, but didn't come to Europe until the 1400s. It is believed that Johan Gutenberg was the first European to use movable type. Before Gutenberg's invention, books in Europe were written by hand, so only a few people owned them or could read them...
>
> After this invention, more books were printed. More people learned to read and write. Printed materials were published and distributed to other cities, so the flow of information and ideas increased...
>
> Today, computers are used more frequently than books are. But it is possible that books may once again become important. A great magnetic force or unknown rays could erase computer records and books will be needed...

Revision

Read through your essay and check for correct word order, correct usage of the passive voice, clear main idea and details, and correct spelling and punctuation. Share your essay with a partner. Your partner should be able to answer the following questions about your essay:

- What is the important invention or discovery?
- When and where was it made?
- Why was this so important?
- Did you use the passive voice correctly?
- Did you use the participles as adjectives correctly?
- Do you have any errors in spelling or punctuation?
- Does the essay need any more information?

Final Draft

Make any changes or additions that are needed in your essay. Then write or type a final copy. You may want to include your final essay in a portfolio of your writing.

Evaluation

Your teacher will grade your essay. You will be evaluated on:

- clarity of ideas and level of supporting detail in your essay;
- correct use and form of passive voice in several tenses; and
- correct use of participles as adjectives.

Unit 10

Sentence Patterns

Before reading about each of these patterns, you first need to learn about clauses.

Clauses
A clause is a group of words with at least one subject and one verb. There are two types of clauses: independent and dependent.

Independent Clause
An independent clause has a subject and verb that form a complete sentence. Place a period or a question mark at the end of an independent clause. Every sentence must have at least one independent clause. **The elderly man jogged in the park.** **Did Henry give $100 to charity?**

Dependent Clause
A dependent clause is an incomplete sentence with a subject and verb. It begins with an adverb, such as *when, after, because, before, although*, and *if*. Every dependent clause must be connected to an independent clause to form a complete sentence. **Because she was sick**, she didn't play in the big game. He left the house **before he ate breakfast.**

Sentence Types

English sentences have three basic patterns: simple, compound, and complex. The type of sentence depends on both the number and the combination of dependent or independent clauses. All sentence types can have single or multiple subjects and single or multiple verbs.

Simple Sentences
A simple sentence has only one clause. Simple sentences can have one or more subjects and more than one verb. Pay particular attention to subject–verb agreement. Sentences with more than one subject take plural verbs. **Han is** a nurse. **Jack and Carol are** late. **You, Kristen, and Sasha are** best friends. I **went** to the store **and walked** the dog yesterday. Eva **needs** new shoes **and wants** a new coat. Charles and Ivan **will send** the package and **pay** for it themselves.

Compound Sentences

A compound sentence is made up of two or more independent clauses (simple sentences). These independent clauses are connected by one of seven coordinating conjunctions, (*and, but, so, or, for, nor, yet*). Compound sentences also can have more than one subject or more than one verb in each clause.

And is used to add information.

The cook prepared the meal **and** the waiters served it to the customers.
Manuel walked right out of the room **and** the other guests and I were shocked.

But and *yet* are used to show contrast.

She always works very hard, **but** she doesn't earn a lot of money.

But is more common than *yet*.

It's already 8:00, **yet** the sun is still shining.

Or is used to show choice.

Either I'm going shopping **or** I'm taking a nap.
His father will bail him out **or** his friend will pay for a lawyer.

So and *for* show causes or results.

Marsha stayed up all night and played cards, **so** she is exhausted.
We could tell the test was very easy, **for** everyone finished early.

Nor connects two negative statements. Note the verb comes before the subject in the second clause.

Harry doesn't eat red meat, **nor** does he eat green vegetables.

Complex Sentences

A complex sentence combines one independent clause and one dependent clause. The clauses can appear in any order. Complex sentences also can have more than one subject or more than one verb in each clause. Different types of dependent clauses begin with different connector words.

Although and *even though* are used to show contrast.
Although Maya is rich, she is not happy.
Patti went to the party **even though** she was sick.

Because is used to show cause and effect.
Because you have done great work, we are giving you a raise.
I like her explanations **because** they are very clear.

Before, after, as soon as, when, and *until* are used to show time relationships.
Before she came to the United States, she lived in Paraguay.
She cried **after** she found out the bad news.
We left **as soon as** the speech was over.

If is used to show the conditional relationship of events.
If you need me, I will always be there for you.
They will come **if** you call them.

Commas in Compound and Complex Sentences

A compound sentence combines two independent clauses with a conjunction. Always insert a comma before the conjunction.

The baby was crying a lot, so Adrian called the doctor.

I don't know Ms. Jackson, but I met her brother Sidney two days ago.

When a dependent clause begins a complex sentence, insert a comma before the independent clause.

As soon as the band stopped, the audience applauded.

After Nestor and I left work, we drove to the movies.

However, the dependent clause also may go after the independent clause. In that case, there is no punctuation between the clauses.

Milt went on vacation although he had little money.   I take a shower before I have breakfast.

■ 10-1 **Punctuation**

Read each sentence below. With a partner, decide if the sentence needs a comma. Insert the comma in the correct place if needed. If no comma is needed, do not write anything.

1. I don't like him because he is a liar.

2. Because my mother drives so fast all the time she gets many speeding tickets.

3. Although he is only 14 years old he is a professional soccer player.

4. I don't like to work the night shift but I have to do it once a month.

5. When Bob gets home from work he usually takes a walk around the block.

6. I tried to cook a fantastic dinner but I burned the meat and the potatoes.

7. Mario loves to talk on the phone and he also spends hours in Internet chat rooms.

8. If Nancy drinks tea or coffee late in the evening she cannot sleep all night.

9. I will go with you if you pay.

10. Samantha often goes to the movies and eats a big tub of popcorn.

■ 10-2 Sentence Writing

Simple Sentences

A. Write three simple sentences to describe the people in your class or school. Write at least one sentence with multiple subjects and verbs.

Example: Alexi is from Russia. Yan and Alexi eat lunch and talk together every afternoon.

1. _____

2. _____

3. _____

Compound Sentences

B. Write four compound sentences about your hobbies. Use *and, but, so,* and *yet.*

Example: I exercise every day, so I am in pretty good shape. I like to sing, and I often go to concerts.

4. (and) _____

5. (but) _____

6. (so) _____

7. (yet) _____

Complex Sentences

C. Write three complex sentences about your morning activities. Use *before, after,* and *as soon as.* Place commas as needed.

Example: Before I leave the house, I wash the dishes. After I wake up, I make my bed.

8. (before) _____

9. (after) _____

10. (as soon as) _____

D. Write three sentences about your classes this semester. Use *although, if,* and *even though.* Place commas as needed.

Example: Although I work hard, I never get an A in geometry.

11. (although) _____

12. (if) _____

13. (even though) _____

■ 10-3 Description of the Illustration

Look at the illustration below. Use it to complete the activities.

A. Write eight sentences describing the illustration. Write a mixture of simple, compound, and complex sentences. Pay particular attention to sentence patterns. You might think of the following questions: Who is in the house? Why is the light on? What is happening in the lighted room? Why is the rest of the house dark?

1. _____

2. _____

3. _____

4. _____

5. _____

6. _____

7. _____

8. _____

B. Think about these questions: Are you ever alone in your house or apartment? Do you ever get nervous? What do you do to calm down when you are nervous? Could you live in the house in the illustration or would you be afraid? Discuss your answers with a partner.

■ 10-4 Communicative Activity

Interview three classmates about their reasons for coming to the United States and attending college. Take notes on their answers in your notebook. Then write sentences describing their choices. If possible, use the conjunctions *and*, *but*, and *so* and the adverbs *because*, *after*, *when*, and *although*.

Classmate #1: _____

_____

_____

_____

_____

Classmate #2: _____

_____

_____

_____

_____

Classmate #3: _____

_____

_____

_____

_____

■ 10-5 Theme-based Discussion

Read each topic below. Make sure you understand the questions. Work in groups of four to discuss the first topic. Choose one person to report the group's answers to the class. Then move to another group to discuss the next topic. Repeat this process until all the topics are discussed. Try to speak to people you haven't spoken to before.

A. People are living longer today, and the problem of taking care of older people is increasing. How are senior citizens cared for in your culture? Who takes care of elderly parents? Is it the first-born? Or the eldest daughter? Do aging parents go to nursing homes? First describe the system in your culture. Then discuss your ideas about the best system.

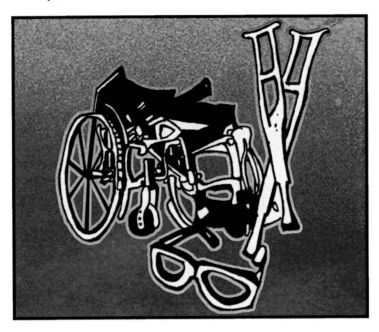

B. In your notebook make a list of the three places in the world you would most like to visit. Write down a few sentences telling why (using complex sentences with *because*). Then compare your list with the lists prepared by the other members of your group.

C. Do you think that the weather affects people's personalities? Are you a warm weather person or a cold weather person? How do you feel in each season? Which season is your favorite? Which is your least favorite? Why?

■ 10-6 Grammar in Action

Read the clauses in Column A. Create complete sentences by matching them with the clauses in Column B. Write the sentences on the lines below. Insert commas if necessary. Then practice reading the complete sentences with a partner.

Column A	Column B
1. _____d_____ I will never go on a date with you	**a.** he saw an accident on the road.
2. _____ Philippina studied all night	**b.** and he hates my brother, too.
3. _____ The flight was delayed	**c.** when she has enough money.
4. _____ My brother can never keep a secret	**d.** because I only think of you as a friend.
5. _____ Barbara will go on vacation	**e.** for my sister to get home from work.
6. _____ While he was driving to school	**f.** but she still got a low grade on the test.
7. _____ He doesn't like me	**g.** because there was a big storm.
8. _____ My mom waited patiently	**h.** so don't tell him that confidential information.

1. _I will never go on a date with you because I only think of you as a friend._ _____

2. _____

3. _____

4. _____

5. _____

6. _____

7. _____

8. _____

Use the story below to complete the activities.

A. Read the story. Circle any coordinating conjunctions or connectors (*and, but, so, when, because,* etc.) and underline any modals you find.

Saturday Disaster

(1) Jack Roman, a businessman, decided to bring work home from the office to do on Saturday. **(2)** He had to pick up his wife from the airport at 5:00. **(3)** He wanted to be comfortable, so he put on very old clothes. **(4)** The shirt had a paint stain, but it was his favorite sweatshirt, made of soft cotton. **(5)** Because he concentrated hard on his work, he didn't notice the time. **(6)** When he looked at the clock, it was 4:30.

(7) He hurried to the car, but he left his wallet on the kitchen table. **(8)** He didn't check the gas gauge of the car because he was paying attention to the road. **(9)** He ran out of gas on the highway near the airport. **(10)** He walked to a gas station one mile from his car. **(11)** He didn't have any money to pay for gas. **(12)** The gas attendant did not believe Jack Roman would pay him back later because Roman wore old clothes. **(13)** When he got back to where his car was supposed to be, he saw it being towed by a tow truck. **(14)** A police officer explained the situation. **(15)** A car cannot be left on the highway, so it was towed to a gas station nearby. **(16)** With the police officer's phone, Jack Roman called a cab at the exit, and he arrived at the airport forty-five minutes late. **(17)** He told the cab driver to wait for him. **(18)** His wife was tired from her long flight, and she was not happy to see her husband in messy clothes. **(19)** He told her about the car and the gas. **(20)** They took a cab to the gas station. **(21)** Jack Roman had to pay $75 for the tow and $20 for the gas. **(22)** He used the cash left over from his wife's trip. **(23)** His wife was very angry at first, but then she began to laugh. **(24)** Jack Roman began to laugh, too. **(25)** He felt very foolish.

B. Carefully read the story again. As you read, decide the sentence type for each sentence: (simple (**S**), compound (**C**), or complex (**X**). Indicate it on the correct line.

1. _____	6. _____	11. _____	16. _____	21. _____
2. _____	7. _____	12. _____	17. _____	22. _____
3. _____	8. _____	13. _____	18. _____	23. _____
4. _____	9. _____	14. _____	19. _____	24. _____
5. _____	10. _____	15. _____	20. _____	25. _____

C. Answer these questions about the passage in complete sentences.

1. What did Jack decide to do on Saturday?

   _____

2. What did he have to do?

   _____

3. Why did he put on a sweatshirt with a paint stain?

   _____

4. Why did Jack Roman leave his house late?

   _____

5. Why did Jack Roman forget his wallet?

   _____

6. Why did Jack forget to check the gas gauge?

   _____

7. What happened to his car on the highway?

   _____

8. Why didn't the gas station attendant believe Jack Roman?

   _____

9. When did he get to the airport?

   _____

10. How did Jack and his wife get to the gas station?

    _____

11. Why did his wife laugh?

    _____

■ 10-8 Sentence Stems

Use the sentence stems below to write simple, compound, or complex sentences. Make sure to have at least one independent clause in each sentence.

1. My three neighbors *are wonderful people.* _____

2. When he heard his fiancée's voice, _____

3. When she hung up the phone, _____

4. After she recovered from her shock, _____

5. Because Mr. Millar is never nice, _____

6. Before I ate dinner, _____

7. He was wearing a painter's hat _____

8. After he got out of jail, _____

9. I forgot to wash my hands _____

10. She always gets in big trouble _____

■ 10-9 Sentence Conclusions

Use the sentence conclusions below to write simple, compound, or complex sentences. Use conjunctions (*and, but, so, yet*) or connectors (*because, when, before, after*). Place commas as needed.

1. _____ she never called me.

2. _____ I just left the restaurant.

3. _____ he came home.

4. _____ he cried for two hours.

5. _____ I got back from vacation.

6. _____ you are not very nice, either.

7. _____ I finish the exam.

8. _____ it rained all night.

9. _____ she comes home after midnight.

10. _____ not tomorrow night.

■ 10-10 Grammar Discussion

A. With a partner, read each sentence below. Circle the subject(s) and underline the verb(s). Then decide which type of sentence it is: simple (**S**), compound (**C**), or complex (**X**). Write the letter on the line.

1. _____S_____ Bob and Joe have three cats and a dog.

2. _____ While I was driving to the beach, I listened to the radio.

3. _____ My mother and father live in Turkey.

4. _____ I work out every day, but I am still overweight.

5. _____ My friend came to my house when he finished work.

6. _____ Sal is a great soccer player, so everyone wants him on the team.

7. _____ Alexi works in a club on weekends, and he is a cook during the week.

8. _____ Although John is lazy, he makes a lot of money.

9. _____ Vincent Van Gogh painted beautiful scenes.

10. _____ If you call me at 2:00 a.m. again, I will not forgive you.

11. _____ Denzel Washington and Halle Barry live in Los Angeles and work in New York.

12. _____ The police officer stopped me, but she didn't give me a ticket.

13. _____ I bought the biology book and the history book, so I have no money left.

14. _____ Hank took a shower after he finished painting the ceiling.

15. _____ Because she is so patient, everyone loves Teresa's mom.

16. _____ A shark attacked a man, and his wife screamed for help.

17. _____ The pilot suddenly died, so Miguel was scared.

18. _____ Becky and Jun are allergic to pencils.

19. _____ Nancy works very hard, yet she is seldom tired.

20. _____ After I washed the dishes, I scrubbed the kitchen floor.

B. Share your answers from Exercise A with the class. Are there any disagreements about sentence types? Explain your decisions for each sentence type.

■ 10-11 The Writing Page

A. Suppose that your friend is having a lot of difficulty in school. She wants to quit college. She sends you an e-mail asking for advice. Try to convince her to stay in school. Give her the best possible reasons why she should get her degree. Use complex sentences with *because* and *if.* Write an e-mail to her on the lines below.

_____

_____

_____

_____

_____

_____

_____

B. Sometimes we do things that are bad for us. We know it, but we do these things anyway. Some people drink too much and others smoke. Some spend too much money. Other people eat too much. Write a paragraph explaining why many people are self-destructive. Use complex sentences with *although, even though,* and *because.*

_____

_____

_____

_____

_____

_____

_____

C. Think about things that make you angry or unhappy. In your notebook, write a paragraph explaining the actions or situations that make this happen. Use complex sentences with *when, after, every time,* and *if.*

■ 10-12 Description of the Photograph

Look at the series of photographs. Use them to complete the activity.

With a partner, tell the story in your notebook in 10 sentences. Use time words (*when, after, before, as soon as*), terms for cause and effect (*because, so*), and contrast terms (*although, even though, but*).

Directed Writing

Task: Write a three-paragraph essay about a life-changing event.

Prewriting

Many people can think of a particular event that changed their lives. Maybe it was a new job, a graduation, or a wedding. Maybe it was a more somber event that forced you to look at the world and life in a different way: 9/11, an earthquake, the loss of a friend or family member. In your notebook, make notes about an event that changed your life or changed the world. Use a chart like the one below.

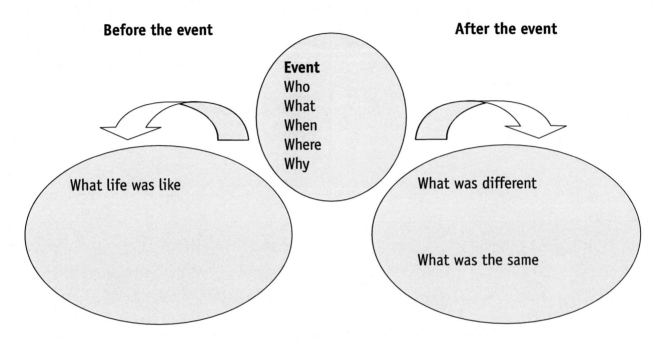

First Draft

Write a first draft of your essay. Use your chart and notes to organize your ideas as you write. Check that your first paragraph describes life before the event. Use the second paragraph to describe the event and its immediate impact. Make sure that your third paragraph concludes the essay, describing later results of the event and how the event changed you or the world. Use compound and complex sentences in several tenses with appropriate conjunctions and connectors.

Model   I remember my life before I got a computer. I had a large typewriter, and I used special tapes and liquids to make corrections on the papers I typed. If I needed to find out some dates or factual information, I would have to go to the library to do research.

Then, one day, I was forced to use a computer. I resisted using it because it seemed so confusing. Until I learned its language and programs, it was hard for me to get anything done.

Now that I have used a computer for so many years, I cannot imagine being without one. As soon as I get up, I turn on the computer. Even though...

Revision

Read through your essay and check for correct usage of dependent and independent clauses, correct usage of conjunctions, clear main idea and details, and correct spelling and punctuation. Share your essay with a partner. Your partner should be able to answer the following questions about your essay:

- What was the event that changed things?
- What was life like before the event?
- How was life different after the event?
- Did you use simple, compound, and complex sentences correctly?
- Did you use different conjunctions and connectors between clauses?
- Do you have any errors in spelling or punctuation?
- Does the essay need any more information?

Final Draft

Make any changes or additions that are needed in your essay. Then write or type a final copy. You may want to include your final essay in a portfolio of your writing.

Evaluation

Your teacher will grade your essay. You will be evaluated on:

- clarity of ideas and level of supporting detail;
- correct use and form of compound and complex sentences; and
- use of different conjunctions and connectors.

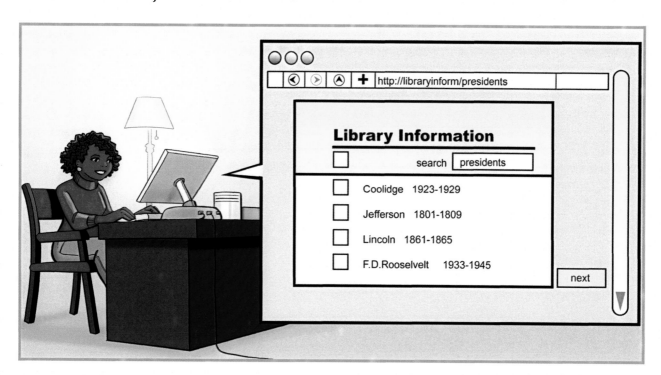

Adjective Clauses

A *clause* is a group of words with a subject and a verb. As you have learned, there are two types of clauses. Independent clauses are complete sentences, and dependent clauses function as a noun, an adverb, or an adjective. Dependent clauses always need to add an independent clause to make a complete sentence.

Placement of Adjective Clauses

Adjective clauses are dependent clauses that act like adjectives. They describe nouns and may appear in three positions: after the subject, after the object of the verb, and after the object of a preposition. Make sure that you always place the adjective clause right after the noun it describes. The verb in the adjective clause must agree in number with the noun it modifies.

1. **adjective clause after the subject**
   Kevin Costner, **who is a Hollywood star,** is most famous for *Dances with Wolves*.
   Our toaster, **which you broke**, fell off the counter.
   The boxes **that we put in the garage** are all wet.

   The clause describes the subject: *Kevin Costner, our toaster, the boxes*.

2. **adjective clause after the object of the verb**
   I called Dan Marino, **who used to be a professional football player.**
   Lila went shopping for a new car, **which she found right away.**
   Every day, Pam and Manolo eat fruit **that is grown without chemicals.**

   The clause describes the object of the verb: *Dan Marino, a new car, fruit*.

3. **adjective clause after the object of a preposition**
   I saw my mother walking in front of the house **where I used to live.**
   We sat behind the man **who always sleeps on the bus.**
   He will make the cake with the brown sugar **that is in the pantry.**

   The clause describes the object of the preposition: *house, man, sugar*.

Adjective clauses begin with relative pronouns (*who, whom, that, which, whose, when, where*).

A. *who, that, which* **as the subject of the adjective clause**
Mary Kay O'Malley, **who works at a vet's office**, loves dogs more than people.
The cold pizza **that I ate** was old and tough, but delicious.

B. *who, whom, that, which,* **(no object) as the object of the adjective clause**
He is the man **whom the cat bit on the finger.**
The steak **that my brother cooked** was as black as coal.
The woman, **who I dated,** has a diamond ring in her nose.
My sister recommended *The Great Gatsby*, **which she read last year.**

C. *when* **and** *where*
I will never forget the day **when Ziggy wore a dress to the Halloween party.**
Morocco is a country **where the food is a mixture of Arabic and French.**

Note: *Where* and *when* are never subjects of a clause. They are always followed by a noun or pronoun and a verb.

D. *whose*
Mohammed Ali, **whose courage was legendary**, now has Parkinson's disease.

Note: *Whose* is possessive, so it must be followed by a noun.

E. **quantity word +** *whom* **or** *which* (*several of whom, two of which,* etc.)
He has read three books, **one of which he stole from an old woman.**
I have two brothers, **both of whom live in San Francisco.**

F. *which* (to modify the whole sentence)
His cat had seven kittens, **which made his small apartment very crowded.**

Reducing an Adjective Clause to an Adjective Phrase

Reducing adjective clauses to adjective phrases is very common, especially in newspaper and magazine articles.

1. **If there is a** *be* **verb in the adjective clause, eliminate the subject and the** *be* **verb.**
   Mr. Harrison, **who is the president of the bank,** was arrested yesterday. *(clause)*
   Mr. Harrison, **the president of the bank,** was arrested yesterday. *(phrase)*

2. **If there is no** *be* **verb, eliminate the subject and change the verb to the** *-ing* **form.**
   My cousin has an apartment **that overlooks the cemetery.** *(clause)*
   My cousin has an apartment **overlooking the cemetery.** *(phrase)*

Placement of Commas in Adjective Clauses

If the information in the clause is necessary for identification, do not place commas around the clause.
The man who married Janna sometimes cries when he looks at his wedding pictures.

If the information in the clause is optional for identification, place a comma before and after the adjective clause.
Professor Jeffreys, who teaches sociology, has written three books and many articles.

If the adjective clause modifies the whole sentence, use *which* and place a comma before the adjective clause.
The plane was late, which meant that we missed our connecting flight.

▪ 11-1 Punctuation

Read the sentences below with a partner. Fill in the blanks with an appropriate relative pronoun (*who, which, that, whose*) and add commas where needed.

1. I know a girl _____ *whose* _____ family is from Somalia.

2. Tony is asking Ana to marry him _____ we all knew would happen.

3. Pomeranians are dogs _____ bark a lot.

4. Mrs. Erenhoffer _____ lived next door was 90 years old last week.

5. Keisha and Jessie have taken classes _____ are quite difficult.

6. The senator is a woman _____ opinion they value.

7. Yusef wants to buy a car _____ is much too expensive.

8. Apples _____ are good for you are also delicious.

▪ 11-2 Sentence Writing

Adjective clauses beginning with *who* or *that* to describe the object

A. Write three sentences describing the kinds of people you don't like.
   Example: I don't like children who are rude. I don't like teachers that give a lot of homework.

   1. _____

   2. _____

   3. _____

Adjective clauses beginning with *who, which,* or *that* to describe the subject

B. Write three sentences describing your classmates and classroom.
Example: The person who sits next to me comes from China. The classroom that we use is in the Currier Building.

4. _____

5. _____

6. _____

Adjective clauses beginning with *whose* to describe the object

C. Use *whose* to write three sentences about the characteristics of people you admire. Remember to follow *whose* with a noun.
Example: I admire people whose family is more important to them than their job.

7. _____

8. _____

9. _____

Clauses with quantity words: *one of which, both of whom,* etc.

D. Write three sentences about your friends or possessions.
Example: I have many international friends, one of whom speaks six languages. I have several CDs, one of which is from Turkey.

10. _____

11. _____

12. _____

Clauses with *which* to describe the general idea of the whole sentence.

E. Write three sentences about your friends and family using *which* to describe the general idea of the previous clause.
Example: I am going to Poland, which makes my grandmother happy.

13. _____

14. _____

15. _____

■ 11-3 Description of the Illustration

Look at the illustration. Use it to complete the activities.

The rock band *Rebirth of Civilization*, which was very popular in the late 1980s, has decided to have a reunion tour. Write sentences to describe the band members, using as many adjective clauses or phrases and possible.

Example: Johnson Cassidy, the drummer who had long blond hair, is now bald.

1. _____

2. _____

3. _____

4. _____

5. _____

6. _____

7. _____

8. _____

9. _____

10. _____

11-4 Grammar in Action

A. Adjective phrases and clauses are often used in newspaper articles. Read the hints in the box to help you recognize them. Can you give more examples of adjective phrases and clauses?

Locating Adjective Clauses and Phrases

1. Look for common or proper nouns followed by a comma in either the object or the subject position.

   Adjective Phrases:
   Anthony Hanson, **the new chief financial officer of Judson Electronics,** is a former Marine.
   The stock price of Compucorp, **one of the richest companies in the world,** dropped more than 27 percent.

   Adjective Clauses:
   Mia Hamm, **who is the world's most famous women's soccer player,** played in the World Cup in 2003.
   The Lion King's songs were written by Elton John, **who also composed the music for Broadway's version of** *Aida.*

2. Look for common nouns followed by present or past participles to indicate adjective phrases.
   The lawyer **appearing on behalf of the store owner** said that his client was acting in self-defense.
   The man **killed in the fire** was the manager of a bagel shop.

3. Look for common or proper nouns followed by *who, when, where, that, which,* and *whose* to indicate adjective clauses.
   Officials in Newark, **which has one of the nation's highest car theft rates,** are clearly perplexed.
   Rap music, which **draws on urban culture and problems,** has been controversial for several years.

B. Now read the newspaper article below. Underline all 18 adjective phrases and clauses in the article.

Sociologists Dispute the Impact of Violent Video Games Played by Teenagers

The debate raging over the impact of video games on teenage behavior continues unabated.

Dr. Marvin Hanson, director of the Center for Research on Teenage Violence, said that there were no clear links between video game violence and teen behavior. "Some parents whose children play Mortal Kombat or Grand Theft Auto, considered the most violent video games on the market, have expressed concerns about aggressive behavior and anxiety in their children," said Dr. Hanson, who has three video-game-playing children of his own.

Harold Levkowitz, an irate parent whose son was assaulted by a fellow student after the two had played Rebel Squadron for five straight hours, said that he wished for a time when teenagers turned to sports to release their aggression. "Kids who don't play soccer or football and have all these pent-up emotions that they just can't release tend to be more in-your-face in their behavior," Mr. Levkowitz, a clinical psychologist, claimed.

Ronda Fleming, 23, an aerobics instructor and lifelong proponent of video games as a way to improve peripheral vision and reaction techniques, stated, "I don't feel that violent video games affect behavior. Kids understand it's just a game they're playing. They won't go around shooting at cars driving by as they do in Grand Theft Auto."

The debate rages on. Meanwhile, young people, whose lives revolve around the video monitor, continue to enjoy the challenges offered by video games.

■ 11-5 Grammar Discussion

Formal vs. Informal Concepts in Adjective Clauses

In a group of four students, read the sentences in the boxes. Discuss differences in levels of formality.

A1.	The woman about whom I was speaking is standing in the corner of the room.
A2.	The person I was talking about is walking out of the room right now.
A3.	The person that I was telling you about would not give me his phone number.
A4.	The guy who I told you about is in my grammar class.

B1.	The book about which I told you was written by Isabel Allende.
B2.	The novel I told you about was written by a Chilean author.
B3.	The work of fiction that I was talking about last night was named *The House of the Spirits*.

C1.	The house in which I was raised was right next to my elementary school.
C2.	The house where I grew up had four bedrooms.
C3.	The house I grew up in had two fireplaces, which was good because the heat didn't work so well.

A. Which sentence in each group is the most formal? Which is the most informal? Why? Does everyone in the group agree?

B. What is the effect of the first sentence in each group? Which one would you use in writing? In speech? Why? Does everyone in the group agree?

C. Discuss the use of the word *whom*. Is it formal or informal? Do members of the group use it in speech or writing? Is the word *whom* still common?

■ 11-6 Theme-based Discussion

Read each topic below. Make sure you understand the questions. Work in groups of four to discuss the first topic. Then choose one person to report the group's answers to the class. Next, move to another group to discuss the next topic. Repeat this process until all the topics are discussed.

A. Everyone has a different personality type. There are people who are shy and people who are confident. Discuss the character traits of shy people and the character traits of confident ones. Which people do you think are generally happier? Why? Could people who appear confident really be shy? How can you tell?

B. Think about how your ideal college would be. Would you prefer a college that is large and diverse, or small and friendly? Tell your group what going to school there might be like, what characteristics it will have, and what characteristics it will not have. Use adjective phrases and clauses if you can.

C. Tell your group about a place that you will always remember. What was it like? Why was it so special?

D. Make a list of three characters in books or movies that you remember well. Explain to your group what made those characters memorable.

■ 11-7 Grammar Practice

A. Read the passage below about Abraham Lincoln, the 16th president of the United States. Circle any words you don't know. Then go back and look them up in a dictionary.

---

(1) Abraham Lincoln was born in a log cabin in Kentucky on February 12, 1809. **(2)** His family later moved to Illinois. **(3)** He was given little formal education. **(4)** Abraham Lincoln walked miles to borrow books and read them by firelight to educate himself. **(5)** He held several jobs in Illinois. **(6)** His law practice in Illinois became successful. **(7)** He had a famous series of debates with Stephen Douglas in 1858. **(8)** He lost to Douglas in the election for senator, but he gained a national reputation. **(9)** He was elected President in 1860. **(10)** In the next year the Civil War began, and he claimed broad executive powers. **(11)** Some people said that these powers were dictatorial. **(12)** He lacked a competent military commander for the Northern Army. **(13)** He suffered through several serious defeats. **(14)** One of these defeats was the first Battle of Bull Run. **(15)** In the Emancipation Proclamation, he declared that slaves were free. **(16)** Military successes helped him gain re-election in 1864. **(17)** Unlike many members of Congress, he wanted to be lenient and forgiving with the southern states after the war. **(18)** John Wilkes Booth shot Lincoln on April 14, 1865. **(19)** Lincoln died the next morning.

B. Now use the sentences in the passage to complete these exercises in your notebook.

1. Choose two sentences from the paragraph and combine them into one sentence by using the relative pronoun with *who*.

2. Change sentence 2 to an adjective clause with *whose*. Then combine it with sentence 1.

3. Change sentence 18 to an adjective clause with *whom*. Then combine it with sentence 19.

4. Choose two sentences from the paragraph and combine them into one sentence by using *which*.

5. Change sentence 11 to an adjective clause with *that*. Then combine it with sentence 10.

6. Change sentence 6 to an adjective clause with *where*. Then combine it with sentence 5.

7. Change sentence 14 to an adjective clause with a quantifier. Then combine it with sentence 13.

11-8 Error Correction

Read the sentences below. There is at least one mistake in each item. The mistakes could be in comma use, relative pronoun choice, or phrase or clause placement. Underline all the mistakes in each sentence, then write the sentence correctly.

1. I used to live in Peru, <u>that is</u> a Spanish-speaking country.

   I used to live in Peru, a Spanish-speaking country.

2. The man who his name is Ali comes from Egypt.

   _____

3. Al Sharpton, who a political leader might run for president.

   _____

4. He never talks to people which have more than five tattoos.

   _____

5. Hetal comes from a place where is very hot all year.

   _____

6. Pele won seven championships who was born in a small town in Brazil.

   _____

7. My mother has an apartment where overlooks that overlooking the park.

   _____

8. I will never forget the day when was my 30th birthday.

   _____

9. Jane who works in a large investment bank which located in southern Connecticut.

   _____

10. Bollywood produces many more movies than Hollywood which is the movie capital of India.

   _____

11. She is the singer that, was discovered in a shopping mall, and that acting in movies now.

   _____

12. The dog which eaten my shoe has an ear that sticking straight up.

   _____

13. My aunt who is the inventor of the "Broccoli is Best!" ad campaign lived to the age of 102.

   _____

A. Read the list of jobs in the box below. What kind of person should do each job? Use both affirmative and negative sentences to discuss the characteristics necessary for the careers in the box. Make sure you use as many adjective clauses as possible in your discussion with the class.

Example: A flight attendant must be someone who is not afraid to fly.

People who have no patience with children should never be pediatricians.

architect	professor	obstetrician	computer specialist	classical pianist
nurse	soccer player	psychiatrist	aerobics instructor	bridge painter
undertaker	stand-up comic	ballet dancer	taxi driver	Starbucks barista
poet	veterinarian	politician	flight attendant	lion tamer

B. Your instructor will provide a newspaper photo to each group of three students. Discuss the people and note their characteristics. Then compose a newspaper article about the people in the photograph. What are they like? What are they doing? Include many adjective clauses and/or phrases.

_____

_____

_____

_____

_____

_____

_____

11-10 Sentence Frames

Complete each sentence. Use the sentence stems below to write statements with adjective clauses or phrases. Make sure the subjects and verbs agree and that you add any needed punctuation.

1. It would be very difficult for me to marry a person _who did not want children._ .

2. My sister bought a dog _____ .

3. The doctor who _____ came from Bangladesh.

4. I will never forget the night _____ .

5. She was quite intrigued by the man whose _____ .

6. Lions _____ are known as the kings of the jungle.

7. Last week Professor Marrocco bought a car _____ .

8. My half-brother went out with a woman_____ .

9. The gift _____ was made of fake, not real, diamonds.

10. Ms. Cooper wore an expensive jade necklace _____ .

11. Pablo Picasso, who _____ , lived many years in Paris.

12. The restaurant _____ served delicious but costly food.

13. _____ which made everyone very happy.

14. Monday is the day_____ .

15. They went to the movies without me, which _____ .

16. Five thousand dollars is the amount_____ .

A. Read the following selection and highlight the adjective clauses.

> My favorite sport is played during the summer. It is a sport that requires nine players on each team. The people who play this sport must be fast, brave, and intelligent. Players who are fast and brave will be able to react quickly to a ball that often travels 90 miles an hour or more. Players who are intelligent will be able to decide what to do before the ball comes to them and will react quickly and correctly even when they cannot watch the other players.
>
> My favorite sport is interesting to watch. People who watch the game have a chance to discuss the strategy of the teams and the quality of the players. Spectators who understand the game well know that they have to watch two places on the field at the same time: the place where the ball is and the place where the runner is. Wise spectators know that the players often make beautiful patterns on the field as they line up to relay the ball in order to catch a runner.
>
> My favorite sport is baseball.

B. On the lines below, write a similar "mystery" composition about your favorite sport, game, or activity. Keep the name of the activity secret until the final sentence. Give as much detail about the activity as possible, and use adjective clauses where you can.

_____

_____

_____

_____

_____

_____

_____

_____

_____

C. When you are finished, read your composition aloud to the class, except for the last line where you say the name of the activity. Other students in the class should try to guess your activity before you give them the answer.

Look at the photograph below. Use it to complete the activities.

A. Describe the two people in the photograph. Who are they? Why are they there? What do you think they are arguing about? Write your answers in your notebook. Use adjective phrases and clauses if you can.

B. What can they do to solve the problem? Whose fault is it when something is wrong between a worker and a customer? Discuss your answers with a partner.

■ 11-13 Unit Review

Directed Writing

Task: Write a three-paragraph essay about a place where you love to spend time.

Prewriting

Is there a particular place that you loved (or still love) to visit and spend time? Maybe your grandmother's kitchen, a pond or swimming hole, a tree house, a favorite restaurant or park, a particular classroom, your first apartment? Close your eyes and picture the place. What do you see? What do you hear? What do you smell? How do you feel? In your notebook, make notes about this particular place. Use a chart like the one below.

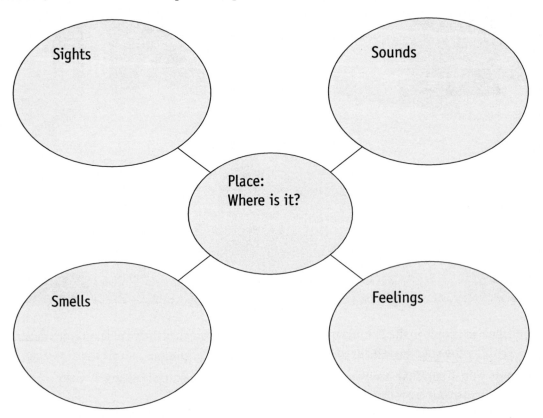

First Draft

Write a first draft of your essay. Use your chart and notes to organize your ideas as you write. Check that your first paragraph identifies the place. Use the second paragraph to describe the sights, sounds, and smells you experience there. Make sure that your third paragraph concludes the essay, stating how you feel in the place and why it is special to you. Use adjective clauses and adjective phrases.

Model When I was young, I loved to spend time in my grandmother's kitchen. Her house, which was only five minutes from ours, was near the woods. I often stopped at her house on my way home from school...

Her kitchen, which was warm and cozy, had a large wood oven. My grandmother always had fresh-baked goods: breads, cakes, and all sorts of wonderful things to eat. I loved to play with her cat, who had a special place on the window near the oven...

In my grandmother's kitchen, my sisters and I were happy. My grandmother always let us take some of the warm cookies that were on the table. Her kitchen was full of love, good food, and wonderful smells, which everyone noticed as they walked past her house...

Revision

Read through your essay and check for correct word order, correct usage of adjective clauses and adjective phrases, correct use of commas, clear main idea and details, and correct spelling. Share your essay with a partner. Your partner should be able to answer the following questions about your essay:

- What place is special to you?
- What is the place like? What do you see, hear, and smell there?
- How does the place make you feel? Why?
- Did you use adjective phrases and clauses correctly?
- Did you use different types of adjective clauses and phrases?
- Do you have any errors in spelling or punctuation?
- Does the essay need any more information?

Final Draft

Make any changes or additions that are needed in your essay. Then write or type a final copy. You may want to include your final essay in a portfolio of your writing.

Evaluation

Your teacher will grade your essay. You will be evaluated on:

- clarity of ideas and level of supporting detail in your essay;
- correct use of adjective clauses and adjective phrases; and
- correct use of commas.

Unit 12

The -*ing* Form and Gerunds

The -*ing* form of a verb can appear in a sentence as one of four parts of speech: a verb, an adverb, an adjective, or a noun. When the -*ing* form appears as a noun, it is called a gerund.

1. **Verb meaning**

   In most sentences, a verb that ends in -*ing* shows a progressive tense (*be* + verb + -*ing*) or perfect progressive tense (*have* + *been* + -*ing*). The two progressive forms can be in present, past, or future time.

   Doug **is mowing** the lawn now. (present progressive)

   Harry **was sleeping** when his mother came home. (past progressive)

   Next Monday, David **will be relaxing** in Cancun. (future progressive)

   Maya **has been living** in a studio apartment on 47th Street. (present perfect progressive)

2. **Adverbial meaning**

   In some sentences, a verb ending in -*ing* is part of an adverb phrase. It is the result of a reduction of an adverb clause to an adverb phrase. In this use, the subject is described *in action* after which another event happens.

   As he **is racing** down the stairs, Dan trips and falls onto the coffee table. (adverb clause)

   Racing down the stairs, Dan tripped and fell onto the coffee table. (adverb phrase)

   While I **was driving** to work, I drank a cup of coffee. (adverb clause)

   Eating an ice-cream cone, the two year-old got chocolate and vanilla all over her new dress. (adverb phrase)

3. **Adjective meaning**

   A verb ending in -*ing* may also appear as an adjective in a sentence. As with other adjectives, it should be placed either immediately before the noun or after a form of the verb *be*.

   The **depressing** news about the war spoiled our good mood.

   I have the most **boring** professor at the college.

   Yelda's new computer is **amazing**.

   Note: The -*ing* form often indicates a cause, while the -*ed* form (past participle) often shows a result.

   The book was fascinating (cause) and kept me interested (result) all night.

4. **Noun meaning**

   In some sentences, the -*ing* form of a verb appears as noun. This -*ing* form is called a gerund. With gerunds, an action becomes an activity.

He will **wed** her in June.	Their **wedding** was in June.
They **met** last week.	Their **meeting** was postponed.
The movie will **end** soon.	The **ending** of the movie was sad.

Gerund as Subject or Object

As with any noun, a gerund in a sentence can be a subject or the object of a verb or of a preposition.

Gerund as the Subject of a Sentence

Swimming is an excellent activity to lose weight.
A poetry **reading** will be held next Friday.

The **beginning** of the class was a lot of fun.

Gerund as the Object of a Verb

Ming went **swimming**.
We don't like **playing tennis**.

Juan prefers **consulting** to **working** for an employer.

There are many verbs that are always followed by gerunds. Some of those involve processes: *avoid, consider, complete, continue, delay, finish, keep, postpone, practice, recall, recollect, remember, resist, risk, start, stop, tolerate, try, understand, comprehend, ponder.*

He **considered moving** to Chicago.
I **don't remember inviting** her to the party.

We **practice speaking** English every day.

Other verbs that are followed by gerunds involve attitudes or feelings: *appreciate, can't bear, can't stand, can't help, dislike, hate, miss, enjoy, like, anticipate, love, mind, prefer, regret, resent.*

They **miss seeing** their grandchildren.
Do you **enjoy sewing and knitting**?

She **prefers walking** in the park when she has free time.

There are also verbs that involve communicating: *admit, advise, deny, discuss, mention, recommend, suggest.*

He **advised taking** all required math courses during freshman year.
I'll **recommend going** out for dinner early tomorrow.

We **suggest planting** bulbs in the spring.

Gerunds also follow phrasal verbs: *think about, talk about, put off, get over, get into, look into, call off, find out about, point out, bring back, give up, go on, fool around with, get through with, sign up for, go back to, go over, keep away from.*

We **put off finding** a new apartment.
Jin **found out about working** in an accounting firm.

I **gave up on getting** tickets for the Jay-Z concert.

Gerund as the Object of a Preposition

We are interested **in learning** about Egyptian art.
Do you ever dream **about becoming a millionaire?**

The boys apologized **for throwing water balloons** at the girls.

Special Uses of Gerunds

A. **Sports Idioms**
   There are two common idioms that describe sports.
   Use *play* + gerund when a ball or puck is part of the game: *play baseball, play hockey, play soccer, play tennis, play football, play basketball.*
   Use *go* + gerund for other sports and activities: *go fishing, go jogging, go swimming, go sailing, go skiing, go shopping* and *go drinking.*

B. **With *give* and *get***

a thrashing	*a beating*	*a spanking*
a tongue-lashing	*a scolding*	

Spelling Rules for *-ing* Forms and Gerunds

The *-ing* is attached to the base form of the word. The spelling of an *-ing* form or gerund depends on the number of vowels and consonants at the end of the word.

1. **for words ending in more than one consonant, add *-ing*.**
   think + -ing = thinking
   build + -ing = building
   finish + -ing = finishing
2. **for words ending in more than one vowel plus a consonant, add *-ing*.**
   cheat + -ing = cheating
   diet + -ing = dieting
   heal + -ing = healing
3. **for words ending in one vowel and one consonant in a stressed syllable, double the consonant and add *-ing*.**
   split + t + ing = splitting
   hem + m +-ing = hemming
   win + n = winning
4. **for words ending in one or more consonants plus *-e*, remove the *-e* and add *-ing*.**
   take + -ing = taking
   write + -ing = writing
   excite + -ing = exciting
5. **for most other words, add *-ing*.**
   study + -ing = studying
   see + -ing = seeing

■ 12-1 Spelling

Use the rules to spell *-ing* forms and gerunds correctly for each word below.

1. give _____*giving*_____   11. take _____

2. stimulate _____   12. shop _____

3. open _____   13. research _____

4. watch _____   14. dig _____

5. read _____   15. bite _____

6. pace _____   16. drive _____

7. sing _____   17. add _____

8. play _____   18. cook _____

9. listen _____   19. fight _____

10. run _____   20. call _____

12-2 Sentence Writing

Find a partner who does not speak your native language. Together, examine the following -*ing* words and phrases. Decide what part(s) of speech these words and phrases can function as. Then write sentences, using them in all of the parts of speech that you can. After you write the sentences, underline each -*ing* word and write in the margin whether the -*ing* word is used as a verb, an adverb, an adjective, or a gerund (noun).

hiding place	writing tablet	engineering	building	fighting
shoveling	cutting board	saying	baking	moving
serving	following	cutting	hiding	writing
interesting	fascinating	swimming	jogging	reading

1. _____

2. _____

3. _____

4. _____

5. _____

6. _____

7. _____

8. _____

9. _____

10. _____

11. _____

12. _____

13. _____

14. _____

15. _____

16. _____

17. _____

18. _____

■ 12-3 Description of the Collage

Before Europeans came to the land that is now the United States, an indigenous population numbering more than 15 million lived on the land. The traditions, culture, and beliefs of Native Americans are great sources of wisdom. Look at the collage below. This collage represents different aspects of Native American life. Use it to complete the activities.

A. In your notebook, write a paragraph describing the collage.

B. Conduct research on the Native American tribes in your area. What tribes lived there? What were their primary activities? Do they still live in the area? In your notebook, write a paragraph telling what you learned.

■ 12-4 Communicative Activity

Interviewing a classmate. Writing a paragraph. Making an oral presentation.

Interview three classmates about their favorite hobbies and activities. Take notes in the table below. In your notebook, write a short paragraph (six–eight sentences) about each classmate. Be prepared to present one of the paragraphs aloud to the class.

Sample questions:

What do you do for fun?
Do you ever go bowling (fishing, hiking, swimming)?
Do you play baseball (basketball, football, soccer)?
What do you do to relax?
Do you work out?
How many times a week?
How much do you walk?
Are you generally an active person or do you lead a sedentary life?

Classmate 1	Classmate 2	Classmate 3

12-5 Theme-based Discussion

Read each topic below. Make sure you understand the questions. Work in groups of four to discuss the first topic. Try to use as many gerunds as you can. Then choose one person to report the group's answers to the class. Next move to another group to discuss the next topic. Repeat this process until all the topics are discussed.

A. Lying is a fairly common activity. Discuss your lying habits. How often do you think you lie? Where are you the most dishonest: in person, on the telephone, in e-mails, or in Internet chat rooms?

B. Which do you like better: to be in water, in the air, or on land? Explain why your element of choice best suits your personality. When you've done this, get a partner and figure out which element best suits your partner and why. Share your views.

C. When it comes to getting dressed, are you a very organized person? That is, for example, do you put your clothes out the night before, so that you don't have to rush or choose in the morning? Do you plan how you will look the next day? Now analyze your drawers and your closet. Does it look like a disaster area or is every item in its proper place? Now think of the area where you keep your shoes. What does it look like? Share your thoughts with the members of your group.

D. The choice of colors sometimes reflects personality. Talk about your own preferences. What is your favorite color? When you buy a new car, what color will it be? When you get all dressed up for a special party, what color do you wear? Does the color of your dress or your shirt show other people the mood that you are in? Discuss color and mood.

12-6 Communicative Activity

A. Friendship is a bond that connects people. Some friendships can last a lifetime. Work together with a partner to describe the two women in the photograph. Where are they? What are they doing? Do you think that they are close friends?

B. Now work by yourself and think about your best friends. What qualities do they have that connect you to them? What activities do you like to do together? Describe a few of your best friends to your partner.

■ 12-7 Error Correction

Read the sentences below. There is at least one mistake in each sentence. The mistakes could be in verb form, subject-verb agreement, preposition, or choice of participle. Underline all the mistakes in each sentence, then write the sentence correctly.

1. I want to playing soccer until I will be 50 years old.

   I will be playing soccer until I am 50 years old.

2. Laura is interested on go to China in vacation next year.

3. The movie was very excited. I was very interesting on it.

4. To eat three slices of cakes are not to good for your healths.

5. While was swimming, I saw two sharks and a dolphin.

6. After go to bed, Henry fall asleep right way.

7. When Narita's father tell story, everybody fall asleep because he is such a bored speaker.

8. I was play soccer when was 15 years old, but now I only shopping for soccer videos.

9. Freddy miss to see his brothers and sisters every days.

10. I really apologize for to hurt your feeling. I will stop to do that. I do promise.

11. Professor Diaz advice to take history before take anthropology.

12. My husband and me discussed to take a train to Chicago because cost fewer money.

13. Oh really! We also talked about to go to Midwest on vacations.

▪ 12-8 Sentence Stems

Use the sentence stems below to write statements with gerunds. Write affirmative and negative statements.

1. Ted can't avoid _____

2. Sally can't understand _____

3. Daisy stopped _____

4. The engaged couple talked about _____

5. Dr. Clement recommended _____

6. It is allows _____

7. They each mentioned _____

8. The court reported _____

9. Janel avoided _____

10. I finally finished _____

11. Morag dislikes _____

12. Song-Hee anticipates _____

13. My neighbor denies _____

14. Anna intends _____

15. Jim loves _____

16. Gabriella enjoys _____

17. Fortunata postponed _____

18. Magdelena suggests _____

19. Mrs. Smith keeps on _____

20. Enid would love _____

■ 12-9 Cloze

In each blank, write the correct form of the verbs in parentheses. The first verb in each pair could be in any tense you have studied so far. The second verb will be a gerund. Make sure your verb tense is correct and gerunds are spelled correctly.

Vacation Dreams

My friends **(1)** _____have discussed going_____ (*discuss/go*) to Bayside resort for three

years. Last week, they **(2)** _____ (*think about/call*) the owner of

a house on the beach, but they **(3)** _____ (*put off/call*) until

today. If they **(4)** _____ (*plan on/go*) to the house this summer,

they have to make their reservation sometime this week. Today they

(5) _____ (*discuss/drive*) all the way up to Maine, where Bayside

resort is. They can reach the resort in eight hours if they **(6)** _____

(*not + think about/stop*). However, if they **(7)** _____ (*consider/fly*)

instead, they **(8)** _____ (*anticipate/get*) there in an hour and a

half. If they go, they **(9)** _____ (*not + resent/have*) members

of their family with them. Between the two of them, they have eighteen relatives who

(10) _____ (*look forward to/spend*) some time in Maine.

All of them say that they **(11)** _____ (*enjoy/fish*) and

(12) _____ (*go/boat*) at the lake nearby. They all

(13) _____ (*like/be*) near the water, too. Well, my friends

(14) _____ (*count on/finish*) their plans by the end of this week.

While they **(15)** _____ (*appreciate/lie*) on the beach, they also

(16) _____ (*think about/eat*) a lot of good seafood. Let's

(17) _____ (*keep/hope*) that their vacation dreams come true!

■ 12-10 **Grammar Practice**

A. With a partner, fill in each sentence with the correct form of one of the words below. Then decide how the form is used: as a progressive verb, an adverb, adjective, or gerund. Write your choice on the line after each sentence.

bark	eat	fish	listen	see	ski	wait	work
charm	excite	give	play	shatter	try	watch	write

1. The _____ glass fell all over the pavement during the accident. _____

2. _____ the baby and the puppy together was a _____ picture. _____

3. Gina is always _____ music when I am _____ to study. _____

4. _____ quickly, the children finished the cookies before their mother came home. _____

5. _____ until the last minute to ask someone out is not a good idea. _____

6. My brother teaches _____ every winter. _____

7. We were _____ an _____ game last night. _____

8. Han and Raj don't like _____ reports. They think _____ speeches is easier. _____

9. _____ is not a very popular sport. _____

10. The neighbor's dogs will be _____ all night. _____

11. _____ intently, Miguel heard the car door slam. _____

12. You have been _____ on that project every night this week. _____

B. Talk about your choices with the class. Did everyone choose the same words for each sentence? Does everyone agree with how each form is used?

■ 12-11 The Writing Page

Write a paragraph of advice for each dilemma. Use appropriate affirmative and negative sentences with the pairings below. Use at least seven of the verb pairs in your paragraphs.

A. A couple finds a dog at their back door. When they examine the dog, they recognize him as belonging to their neighbors, who live six houses down the street. Every time they have taken a walk in the neighborhood, no matter the weather, they have seen this dog chained to a post outside the neighbor's house. On even closer examination, they discover that the dog is very skinny and is limping. What can, and what should, and what must this couple do?

put off/discuss	consider/call	keep on/watch
stop/worry	talk about/confront	suggest/arrest
forget/care	start/call	discuss/adopt

_____

_____

_____

_____

_____

_____

_____

B. Tina Black has worked in the same office for four years. She doesn't like most of the people in her office although she has a few friends. She is forty years old, she enjoys a good salary, she thinks that she is too young to stay in a job that she doesn't like. She is afraid to change jobs, however, because she enjoys a good salary.

begin/look	enjoy/do	forget/dream
postpone/make	try/find	understand/feel
quit/complain	anticipate/get	complete/work

_____

_____

_____

_____

_____

_____

_____

■ 12-12 Description of the Photograph

Look at the photograph. Use it to complete the activities.

A. Write a paragraph describing what is going on in the photograph, entitled "Tango Argentino."

_____

_____

_____

_____

_____

_____

_____

B. Dancing is a very enjoyable activity. In your notebook, write about your interest (or lack of interest) in dancing. What kind of music do you like to dance to? Where do you go to dance? Did you like to dance more in the past than now?

Directed Writing

Task: Write a three-paragraph essay describing your favorite pastimes and hobbies.

Prewriting

Think of your three favorite free-time activities. They may be sports activities, such as bowling or playing soccer. Or they may be quieter activities, such as collecting stamps or reading. In your notebook, list the activities and write as many details as you can about each one. Use idea maps like the ones below.

Activity   **Details**

_____ing _____

_____ing _____

_____ing _____

First Draft

Use your prewriting notes to write a first draft of your essay. Use gerunds:

- as the subject of sentences (*Listening to classical guitar is very relaxing.*).
- as the object of prepositions (*I'm looking forward to seeing the concert.*)
- as the object of verbs (*I enjoy going to Washington.*)
- after *go*, to talk about recreational activities (*Let's go dancing.*)
- and after special expressions, such as *spend time, have trouble*, and so on (*I have trouble understanding British movies.*)

Include as much information as you can about your favorite free-time activities and why you enjoy them so much. Make sure your first paragraph mentions each of the three activities. Don't forget to indent the first line and write the main idea sentence at the beginning of each paragraph.

> **Model** Some of my favorite free-time activities are playing baseball on Saturday mornings, reading interesting historical novels, and cooking for my friends. I really enjoy playing baseball because . . .
> I have always liked reading historical novels, especially . . .
> I like to spend time cooking for my friends, but I don't often . . .

Revision

Read through your essay and check for gerunds used as the subject of the sentence, the object of prepositions, the object of particular verbs, and after *go,* to talk about recreational activities. Pay particular attention to special expressions that are followed by gerunds. Don't forget to use other *-ing* forms such as adjectives. Share your essay with a partner. Your partner should be able to answer the following questions about your essay:

- What are your favorite free-time activities?
- What do you enjoy about these activities?
- Did you use gerunds in several different ways?
- Did you use other *-ing* forms correctly?
- Do you have any errors in spelling or punctuation?
- Does the essay need any more information?

Final Draft

Make any changes or additions that are needed in your essay. Then write or type a final copy. You may want to include your final essay in a portfolio of your writing.

Evaluation

Your teacher will grade your essay. You will be evaluated on:

- clarity of main ideas and level of supporting detail in your essay,
- use of gerunds and *-ing* forms in the correct context, and
- appropriate use of special expressions that are followed by gerunds.

Common Verbs with Irregular Past and Past Participle Forms

base	past	past participle	base	past	past participle
be	was/were	been	leave	left	left
become	became	become	lend	lent	lent
begin	began	begun	let	let	let
bite	bit	bitten	lose	lost	lost
break	broke	broken	make	made	made
bring	brought	brought	mean	meant	meant
build	built	built	meet	met	met
buy	bought	bought	pay	paid	paid
catch	caught	caught	put	put	put
choose	chose	chosen	quit	quit	quit
come	came	come	read	read	read
cost	cost	cost	ride	rode	ridden
cut	cut	cut	ring	rang	rung
dig	dug	dug	rise	rose	risen
do	did	done	run	ran	run
draw	drew	drawn	say	said	said
drink	drank	drunk	see	saw	seen
drive	drove	driven	sell	sold	sold
eat	ate	eaten	send	sent	sent
fall	fell	fallen	shake	shook	shaken
feed	fed	fed	shoot	shot	shot
fight	fought	fought	shut	shut	shut
find	found	found	sing	sang	sung
fly	flew	flown	sleep	slept	slept
forget	forgot	forgotten	speak	spoke	spoken
freeze	froze	frozen	spend	spent	spent
get	got	gotten	stand	stood	stood
give	gave	given	steal	stole	stolen
go	went	gone	sweep	swept	swept
grow	grew	grown	swim	swam	swum
have	had	had	take	took	taken
hear	heard	heard	teach	taught	taught
hide	hid	hidden	tell	told	told
hit	hit	hit	think	thought	thought
hold	held	held	throw	threw	thrown
hurt	hurt	hurt	wake	woke	woken
keep	kept	kept	win	won	won
know	knew	known	write	wrote	written
lead	led	led			

Common Adverbs in Time Clauses

1. **For an action that has happened, use *already*.**

   I **have already paid** my phone bill this month.
   The Yankees **have already won** three games against the Red Sox this season.
   Kimberly **has bought** three sweaters during the Macy's winter sale **already**.

2. **If the action hasn't happened, use *still* or *yet*. Using *still* implies that the action should have happened earlier.**

   I **haven't seen** the cat **yet** this morning.
   Alex **still hasn't sent** in the order for our new furniture.
   We **haven't picked out** the flowers for her wedding **yet**.

3. **If you are asking a question about an anticipated action in a set period of time, use *yet*.**

   Have you **sold** your house **yet**?
   Has your lazy cousin **gotten** a job **yet**?
   Have they **found** the car keys **yet**?

4. **If you expect a condition or action to continue into the future, use *so far*.**

   I **have changed** my oil 6 times **so far** this year.
   So far, my brother **has bought** his girlfriend a diamond ring, a Movado watch, and a Porche, but she still won't marry him.
   We've **scored** twice **so far** this quarter.

5. **in expressions with *for* and *since***

   a. *For* can begin phrases that express a period of time. These phrases "add up" time. They can appear at the beginning or the end of a sentence.

      Sarah **has been** in love with Ben **for** an hour.
      For six months, we **have waited** for this day to arrive.

   b. *Since* begins phrases and clauses that "point to" the beginning of a time period. They can appear at the beginning or the end of a sentence.

      Jane **has had** trouble sleeping **since** the earthquake of 1995.
      Since that new boy came to our school, Marta **has worn** lipstick every day.

Note: When the main clause is in present perfect tense, the *since* time clause will be in simple past. It is incorrect to write: They have donated blood since they have been in high school.

Answer Key

Answers are provided here for those activities that require specific answers. Answers will vary in all other activities. For each Unit Review/Directed Writing task, your instructor will provide feedback on your essay.

UNIT 1: THE PRESENT TENSE: SIMPLE AND PROGRESSIVE
■ Activity 1-1 (page 10)

Base Form	3rd Person Singular	/s/	/z/	/ɪz/
stop	stops	X		
wait	waits	X		
miss	misses			X
sleep	sleeps	X		
go	goes		X	
read	reads		X	
drive	drives		X	
start	starts	X		
pass	passes			X
love	loves		X	
point	points	X		
type	types	X		
play	plays		X	
watch	watches			X
want	wants	X		
talk	talks	X		
need	needs		X	

■ Activity 1-6 (page 15)
2. is driving
3. works
4. has
5. is using
6. has
7. studies
8. need
9. wash
11. works
12. am thinking
13. are having
14. is studying
15. prefers
16. is wearing
17. knows
18. likes

■ Activity 1-9 (page 18)
1. John is having a party this Saturday night.
2. Bruce and Bob love to play chess. They are very good players.
3. Do you want to go to a club with me tomorrow night?
4. Marco doesn't want to go to his mother-in-law's house, but he is going anyway,
5. Do you smell burned bread? I hate that smell.
6. Why do you always yell at the dog? He is just an animal.
7. I always write in my journal before I go to bed.
8. This fall, I am going to look at the beautiful leaves.
9. I don't like apple pie. It's too sweet.
10. I always listen to music when I am cleaning the house.
11. When are you leaving? Is your brother going with you?
12. Right now, Paul is living in Florida with his parents.
13. Quincy eats too much, so he is very fat now.

UNIT 2: THE PAST TENSE: SIMPLE AND PROGRESSIVE
■ Activity 2-1 (page 26)
1. Last weekend⌢Marco went to the movies.
2. While we were watching the game⌢she ordered a pizza.
3. As soon as they saw their grades⌢Anna and Luke called their parents to celebrate.

4. The bookstore was very crowded when I arrived.
5. Peter didn't realize his book was gone until he got to class.
6. In September 2003⌢I was traveling around Thailand.

■ Activity 2-4 (page 29)
Sequence A
12 We eventually decided to just stay home and enjoy the fire.
10 We decided that we wanted to be alone.
6 We made some coffee.
4 We thought about making a fire and staying home.
11 We discussed going to a movie.
2 We saw that the weather would be cold and rainy.
1 We woke up unusually early that day.
7 We looked through the newspaper to find the movie section.
5 We sat down to drink the coffee and decide how to spend the day.
8 We saw an advertisement for an auction that day.
9 We planned to call our friends to join us.
3 We ate some bagels with cream cheese.

Sequence B
6 Anatoly wanted to take the train.
10 They looked at hundreds of paintings.
8 Anatoly looked forward to seeing the Byzantine exhibition.
11 They decided to have lunch.
3 They often visited the Moscow art museums.
4 They planned to go to the Metropolitan Museum of Art on Fifth Avenue.
12 They ate at the Museum coffee shop.
5 Ludmilla wanted to drive into the city.
1 Anatoly and Ludmilla decided to go to New York City for the day.
2 They lived most of their lives in Russia.
7 Ludmilla looked forward to seeing the Impressionists.
10 They thought about strolling through the streets of Moscow.
13 They discussed the paintings they had seen.
14 They got very tired.
9 They walked for over a mile through the museum.
15 They had a great day.

■ Activity 2-8 (page 33)
1. While Sam was driving to school, he saw an accident.
2. Last month, Professor Jacobson found a wallet in the student center.
3. When Marta finished the book last night, she took a break.
4. Helga was born in 1981. She spent her youth in a small town where her mother taught.
5. Nancy Rosen kept her name after she got married last year.
6. Horace quit his job when he found out that everyone got a raise but him.
7. Someone stole the bag that Yeng Yu hid under the table.
8. The students wrote paragraphs while the professor was correcting their grammar tests.

■ Activity 2-9 (page 34)
I **will** never **forget** Professor Schlessingham, who **taught** Medieval Literature at a university in New York City. I should not **say** that he **was** egotistical, uncreative, antisocial, uncaring, and boring, that he **didn't care** about students. But I **will tell** a story **to illustrate** my point.

It **was** a snowy Monday morning in February. The snow **started** at 6:00 the night before, and by 11:00 a.m. the next day, there **were** more than two feet on the ground. Since the school **was** in New York and most people either **walked** or **took** the subway, it never **closed** for snow. Professor Schlessingham **lived** in Connecticut, 75 miles away. There **was** no way that he **was coming**.

I **lived** in a dormitory on campus, and the classroom building **was** twenty yards away. I **left** my nice, warm room and **walked** into the storm. I couldn't **see** three feet ahead because of the wind and snow. The class **started** at 11:30. When I **walked** into the classroom, I **turned on** the lights and **sat** in the middle of the room. I never **expected to see** anyone that day.

I **took out** my book. It **was** *Beowulf,* an old English poem. When I **heard** the weather forecast the day before, I **didn't read** the book. At 11:35 a.m., I **looked** out the window. It **was** still **snowing** hard. Just at that moment, the door **opened** and a snowman **came in**. He **walked** in and **took off** his coat and hat, and **took** his position in front of the room. It **was** Professor Schlessingham. I **couldn't believe** it. He **took out** his old yellow notes and **started to read** in his dry monotone. Every five minutes or so he **looked up** and **asked**, "Any questions?" Since I **had** no idea what the book **was** about, I **stayed** quiet. This **continued** for almost an hour. Finally, he **put away** his notes, **walked** to the corner of the room, **put on** his coat and hat, and **left**. He **didn't look** at me or **say** a word to me—about the weather or about the fact that I **was** the only student in the class.

The next Wednesday the class **was** filled with students. Professor Schlessingham **walked** into the room, **took out** the old yellow notes and **said**, "Let's continue our discussion of *Beowulf*." One of the students **raised** his hand, "Professor, what do you **mean**, 'continue'? We **didn't** even **start talking** about *Beowulf*. We **were** supposed to start on Monday, but that **was** the day of the snowstorm." Professor Schlessingham **said**, "We **had** class Monday." All the students **replied**, "Are you **kidding**? It **snowed** three feet! How many students **came**?" Professor Schlessingham **said**, "I **don't know**. We **discussed** the beginning and middle of the poem. **Get** notes from the students who **were** here!" Everyone **looked** around the room and **asked** "**Were** you here?" "Who **was** stupid enough **to come** out in the snow for a class?"

I **said**, "I **was** the only one here, but I **didn't take** any notes." "What an idiot," they all **yelled** at me. So instead of getting credit for coming to class, I only **made** my fellow students angry at me. "Too bad for all of you," **said** Professor Schlessingham. We never **talked** about the beginning or middle of *Beowulf*, and we even **had** a test the next class about the parts everyone **missed**. Needless to say, everyone **failed** the test, including me, which **made** Professor Schlessingham extremely happy.

■ Activity 2-10 (page 35)
Alarm

Last month, it snowed for three days. Then the temperature dropped and there **(1) was** a sheet of solid ice on the ground and the roads. On the second day, I **(2) was driving** to work on Lincoln Avenue when my car **(3) spun** out of control and **(4) began** to circle around. I **(5) screamed**. Finally I **(6) got** control of the car again.

After I **(7) arrived** at college, I **(8) heard** that classes **(9) were meeting** that day, so I **(10) prepared** my notes for class. While I **(11) was planning** my class, four students from the class **(12) came** to my office and **(13) said** that they **(14) wanted** to go home because of the weather.

While we **(15) were discussing** whether we should stay or go home, an alarm bell **(16) rang**, so we all **(17) left** the building and **(18) waited** for the alarm to stop ringing. We **(19) shivered** the whole time we **(20) waited** for the bell to stop. Finally, the bell **(21) stopped,** and we **(22) decided** to go home.

Later that week, several students were absent. Then I **(23) woke up** one morning that week with a very sore throat. It turns out that all

of us **(24) had** the flu for two weeks. While we **(25) were lying** in bed with the flu, we **(26) wondered** why the college was open on that fateful day of the ringing alarm bell.

UNIT 3: THE FUTURE TENSE
■ Activity 3-1 (page 42)
1. As soon as he is promoted, David will get a big raise. OR David will get a big raise as soon as he is promoted.
2. When we are on vacation, Mike and I are going to visit our parents. OR Mike and I are going to visit our parents when we are on vacation.
3. If Li gets the job, he will not quit school. OR Li will not quit school if he gets the job.
4. Until you improve your grades, you will need to study every day. OR You will need to study every day until you improve your grades.
5. If it is going to snow, Mark and Gonzalo won't go to class. OR Mark and Gonzalo won't go to class if it is going to snow.
6. When Jen and I go shopping, we will probably spend a lot of money. OR Jen and I will probably spend a lot of money when we go shopping.
7. Before I start my paper, I will research several topics. OR I will research several topics before I start my paper.
8. After Helen comes home from work, she will make dinner for everyone. OR Helen will make dinner for everyone after she comes home from work.

■ Activity 3-9 (page 50)
For as long as he can remember, Eddie has wanted a pet. Now that he is ten, his parents have finally said that he can have one. Now he has to think about what kind of pet to get. His mother has said that it is critical that his pet is easy to train. She doesn't care whether he **gets** a dog, a puppy, a cat, a kitten, a guinea pig, a rabbit, or even a ferret, but the pet must be trainable or kept in a cage. His mother doesn't **plan to clean up** after a messy pet. Eddie **hopes to be able to go** to an animal shelter **this** weekend. He **wants** to see all of the animals that are available for adoption before he **makes up** his mind. Once he **sees** the adult and the baby animals, he **will know** whether he **wants** a baby that he intends **to train** himself, or an adult that he won't have to train. It is important that he holds the animals one by one. He **is planning to spend** a lot of time at the animal shelter so that he will be able to observe the "souls" of the animals. He has decided that whichever pet he chooses, the pet **will connect** with his own soul.

■ Activity 3-10 (page 51)
1. Harriet hopes to be able to finish her career on a high note.
2. I will have a soda.
3. It is important that you understand my problems.
4. We will go out to dinner tonight if he gets paid today.
5. My neighbors are going to move in June.
6. I want to be able to create an account for my daughter.
7. Aaron and Renee are getting married next month.
8. I plan to mail their wedding gift out to California tomorrow.

UNIT 4: QUESTIONS
■ Activity 4-1 (page 58)
1. What did Kayla do after work yesterday?
2. Are you and I going to fight all night?
3. Was the class full when Sayed arrived?
4. Could you please lend me your calculator?
5. If the library is closed, where will they go?
6. Do I need all those books for this project?
7. Were they planning to go to the concert early?
8. Should Steve come to the professor's office now?

Activity 4-7 (page 64)

1. What is Robert doing tomorrow at 3:30?
2. What time does the game start? I think it starts at nine o'clock.
3. Where are they from? Are they from Colombia?
4. Does he work in a pharmacy? He makes a good salary.
5. Can you tell me what time it is?
6. Do Victoria and I have to go to school today?
7. Where were they shopping this morning? At the grocery and the mall.
8. Would you lend me a book, please?
9. Why does Mosi work two jobs? To pay for school.
10. When did Chiang go to class? When you were sleeping.
11. What was the weather like yesterday? Was it cold?
12. Doesn't Horacio have a red car? No, he doesn't. He has a green one.
13. Does he know the professor's name?

UNIT 5: PRESENT PERFECT AND PRESENT PERFECT PROGRESSIVE

Activity 5-7 (page 80)

Maria is a professional photographer. When she (1) **came** here five years ago from France, she (2) **didn't know** a lot about photography. But she (3) **studied** at a famous school in San Francisco after she (4) **arrived** in this country. Now Maria's specialty is wildlife. She (5) **takes** photographs of wild animals. She (6) **has sold** many of her pictures to different magazines since she (7) **started** doing this work. So far, she (8) **has traveled** to Africa and Brazil, but she (9) **hasn't visited** India yet. Several times, she (10) **has had** problems doing this kind of work. For example, a large animal almost (11) **killed** her in Africa. Clearly, Maria (12) **has lived** an exciting life.

Right now, Maria (13) **is working** on a project for *National Geographic Magazine*. For several weeks, she (14) **has taken** pictures of bears in the Rocky Mountains. Last week, while she (15) **was studying** a mother bear with her babies, she (16) **saw** several snakes, so she (17) **took** some pictures of them, too. As soon as Maria (18) **has finished** her project on the bears, she (19) **will go back** to Africa to photograph elephants.

UNIT 6: MODALS

Activity 6-1 (page 90)

1. **F** You [ɔtə] to take Bus 24.
2. **H** It's 10:25.
3. **G** No, I [kʊdnt]. I left my book in the classroom.
4. **D** I don't know yet. I haven't decided.
5. **B** Sure, here you are.
6. **E** They're on your head.
7. **A** Sorry, I [kænt]. I hurt my back yesterday.
8. **C** Well, I [kən] write programs and use Photoshop®.

Activity 6-7 (page 96)

Statues of Chac Mool, a strange human figure, are found in Toltec temples in Mexico and Central America. Carlos Fuetes wrote a story about a man, Filiberto, who bought a Chac Mool statue.

Sunday: My friend Pepe knows that I collect statues. He said that I (1) _ought to_ look at a statue of Chac Mool in a little antique shop. The stone doesn't look so old, so the statue (2) **may** not be authentic. The shopkeeper insists that it is. I suppose it (3) **could** be real, but I doubt it. I bought it anyway and moved it back to my house. It's in the basement right now, but it really (4) **ought to** be displayed in the sunlight.

Monday: You (5) **should** have seen the mess in the basement. The water pipes broke last night. I (6) **may** have left the water running in the kitchen and now the basement is full of water. The statue is all right, but I (7) **could** not get to work on time because the plumbers (8) **could** not get here right away.

Wednesday: I (9) **couldn't** sleep much last night. I heard some strange sounds and the pipes broke again. In addition, it rained last night and all the rainwater got into the basement!

Thursday: I (10) **may** have to sell the house if these problems continue. I (11) **can** scrape moss off Chac Mool because the basement is so damp. I really (12) **should** move the statue upstairs.

Friday: Last night Chac Mool came into my bedroom! (13) **Can** anybody help me? I (14) **can't** believe all of this….

Saturday: I (15) **can't** continue living in this house with all the water. I (16) **ought to** get out of here now…

Activity 6-9 (page 98)

1. If you want to get a raise, you'd better start working harder.
2. Would you please turn down the radio? I can't concentrate with that classical music.
3. This weekend, I might go to the beach, or I could go to the museum.
4. Could I speak with Sigmund?
5. Julie is coming from Korea. She may speak Korean.
6. Gultekin may be from Turkey or from Jordan. I'm not sure.
7. You shouldn't be quiet about the broken vase. Dad will be very angry.
8. My brother works in an appliance store, so I can get a discount on a microwave.
9. Ty and Mohammed could have been at the movies.
10. Sascha may ask the professor.
11. Will I be able to see the dress?
12. We'd better leave early; it's snowing.

UNIT 7: IMPERATIVES AND MODALS OF NECESSITY, OBLIGATION AND PROHIBITION

Activity 7-1 (page 106)

1. **D** No, we don't have to stop, unless you need something.
2. **F** No, but he likes to.
3. **H** Yeah, I had to walk her, and it was raining!
4. **E** I have to have it loud if I want to hear the music.
5. **G** In the library. She has to study.
6. **C** They have to talk to the teacher.
7. **B** I've got to go to class.
8. **A** Yes, we've got to eat it. My grandmother made it.

Activity 7-7 (page 112)

Suggested answers. Other logical answers are possible.
Water the plants.
Get the mail.
Feed the cat.
Lock the door.
Turn off the television.
Clean the bathroom.
Pay the bills.
Don't use the computer.
Do the laundry.
Don't drive the car.
Take notes for me in class.
Don't buy the groceries.

Activity 7-8 (page 113)

1. I must read in English every day.
2. Don't run across the street, please.
3. Mr. Grossman doesn't have to lecture this week.
4. Finish the project tonight.
5. She has got to win the game.
6. Do not let the dog out.
7. Kelley didn't have to work last summer.
8. Drink your milk!
9. Raj has got to call his mother.
10. Let's have pie for dessert.

Activity 7-10 (page 115)

In Greek mythology, Zeus was the most important god. There was no sickness, no hunger, and no sorrow. There were no problems at all.

But Zeus was not happy when man learned how to use fire. He called the other gods. "We (1) _have to_ do something. We (2) **must** punish man for using fire. (3) **Let's** create a woman. She (4) **has to** be beautiful so man will not be suspicious.

So the gods created Pandora and sent her to Earth. Epimethus saw this beautiful woman and thought, "This (5) **must** be my lucky day!" He walked over to her and said, "(6) **Let's** go for a walk." Pandora and Epimethus were happy. They (7) **didn't have to** work much.

One day, Mercury arrived carrying a beautiful box. "I (8) **have to** put this heavy box down. Can I leave it here?" Pandora said, "Of course, but you (9) **must** stay for dinner. Mercury declined, and said that he'd be back soon. Then he added, "(10) **Don't touch** that box." Pandora and Epimethus agreed.

Pandora was curious about the beautiful box. But Epimethus reminded her, "(11) **Stay** away from the box. Pandora kept looking at the box. She heard voices inside the box. "(12) **Open** the box. Let us out."

So she opened it just enough to peek inside. A swarm of hideous, winged creatures flew out. Evil, sickness, and serious problems had escaped into the world. But then she heard one more voice coming from inside the box. She opened the box and found Hope inside. So to this day, even though there are serious problems all over the world, people (13) **have to** hold on to hope.

UNIT 8: THE NOUN PHRASE

Activity 8-1 (page 122)

1. beautiful huge new downtown office
2. her green and white striped sweater
3. their dirty old cramped apartment
4. three gorgeous tall strong leafy trees
5. a fascinating long mystery story
6. shy young skinny orange cat
7. large rowdy unpredictable loud class
8. several sleek modern expensive compact phones

Activity 8-5 (pages 126-127)

A.

When **King Arthur** reigned, there lived in **the county** of **Cornwall**, **a farmer** who had **a son** named **Jack**. He was very smart with **a quick wit**. No one could defeat him.

In **those days, Mount Cornwall** was guarded by **a huge giant** named **Cormoran**. He was **eighteen feet** tall and about **nine feet** around. He had **a fierce, grim face** and was **the terror** of **all the nearby towns and villages**. He lived in **a cave** in **the rugged mountain**. Whenever he wanted **food**, he would wade over to **the mainland** where he would take for himself **whatever he wanted**. When **people** saw him, they ran out of **their houses**. He took **their cattle** and carried **a dozen oxen** on **his back** at a **time**. He tied **the sheep and hogs** around **his waist**. He had done this for **so many years** that **all of Cornwall** despaired.

One day, Jack was in the **town hall** when **the members** of the **town council** were discussing **the giant**. **The poor young lad** asked: "What **reward** will be given to **the man** who kills **Cormoran**?"

"**The giant's treasure** will be **the reward**," they said.
"Then I'll do it," said **Jack**.

Jack got **a horn, shovel, and an axe**. He went to **Mount Cornwall** just as it started to get dark. Before morning, he had dug **a pit** twenty-two feet deep and nearly as wide, and covered it with **long sticks and straw**. Then he spread **a little mold** over the **sticks and straw** so that it looked like **plain ground**. **Jack** then sat on **the opposite side** of **the pit**, farthest away from **the giant's cave**. At **sunrise**, he put **the horn** to **his mouth** and blew, *Tantivy, Tantivy.* **This noise** woke up **the giant**, who rushed from **his cave** crying: "**You horrible man**, you have disturbed **my rest!** You shall pay dearly for this. I will take you whole and broil you for **breakfast!**" But just as he finished speaking, **the giant** tumbled into **the pit**. **The mountain** shook when he fell. "Oh, **Giant**," said Jack, "where are you now? Oh, look, you've fallen into **Lob's Pound**. What do you think now of broiling me for **your breakfast?** Will **no other diet** serve you but **poor Jack?**" After **Jack** teased **the giant** for **a while**, he hit **the giant** on **the head** with **his axe**, and killed him on **the spot**.

Jack then filled up **the pit** with **earth** and went to search **the giant's cave**. He found **a fortune** in **treasure**. When **the council** heard of **the giant's death**, they presented **Jack** with **a sword and a belt**. They were embroidered in **gold** with **these words**: "Here's **the brave Cornish man** who slew **the giant Cormoran.**" **The council** declared that from **that day forward**, he would be known as **Jack the Giant Killer**.

B.

King Arthur: Subject
the county: Object of a Preposition
Cornwall: Object of a Preposition
a farmer: Subject
a son: Object of a Verb
Jack: Object of a verb
a quick wit: Object of a Preposition
those days: Object of a Preposition
Mount Cornwall: Subject
a huge giant: Subject
Cormoran: Object of a Verb
eighteen feet: Object of a Verb
nine feet: Object of a Verb
a fierce, grim face: Object of a Verb
the terror: Object of a Verb
all the nearby towns and villages: Object of a Preposition
a cave: Object of a Preposition
the rugged mountain: Object of a Preposition
food: Object of a Verb
the mainland: Object of a Preposition
whatever he wanted: Object of a Verb
people: Subject
their houses: Object of a Preposition
their cattle: Object of a Verb
a dozen oxen: Object of a Verb
his back: Object of a Preposition
a time: Object of a Prepositon
the sheep and hogs: Object of a Verb
his waist: Object of a Preposition
so many years: Object of a Preposition
all of Cornwall: Subject
One day: Object of a Verb
Jack: Subject
the town hall: Object of a Preposition
the members: Subject
the town council: Object of a Preposition
the giant: Object of a Verb
he poor young lad: Subject
reward: Object of a Verb
the man: Object of a Preposition
Cormoran: Object of a Verb
The giant's treasure: Subject
the reward: Object of a Verb
Jack: Subject
Jack: Subject
a horn, shovel, and an axe: Object of a Verb
Mount Cornwall: Object of a Preposition

a pit: Object of a Verb
long sticks and straw: Object of a Preposition
a little mold: Object of a Verb
the sticks and straw: Object of a Preposition
plain ground: Object of a Verb
Jack: Subject
the opposite side: Object of a Preposition
the pit: Object of a Preposition
the giant's cave: Object of a Preposition
sunrise: Object of a Preposition
the horn: Object of a Verb
his mouth: Object of a Preposition
This noise: Subject
the giant: Object of a Verb
his cave: Object of a Preposition
You horrible man: Subject
my rest: Object of a Verb
breakfast: Object of a Preposition
the giant: Subject
the pit: Object of a Preposition
The mountain: Subject
Giant: Subject
Jack: Subject
Lob's Pound: Object of a Preposition
your breakfast: Object of a Preposition
no other diet: Subject
poor Jack: Object of a Verb
Jack: Subject
the giant: Object of a Verb
a while: Object of a Preposition
the giant: Object of a Verb
the head: Object of a Preposition
his axe: Object of a Preposition
the spot: Object of a Preposition
Jack: Subject
the pit: Object of a Verb
earth: Object of a Preposition
the giant's cave: Object of a Verb
a fortune: Object of a Verb
treasure: Object of a Preposition
the council: Subject
the giant's death: Object of a Preposition
Jack: Object of a Verb
a sword and a belt: : Object of a Preposition
gold: Object of a Preposition
these words: Object of a Preposition
the brave Cornish man: Object of a Verb
the giant Cormoran: Object of a Verb
The council: Subject
that day forward: Object of a Preposition
Jack the Giant Killer: Object of a Verb

Activity 8-8 (page 130)
1. My cat loves to sleep on the couch.
2. The book on the table is Henry's.
3. Her red shoes are perfect for dancing.
4. My tall brother is really a good cook. He is always in the kitchen.
5. Hilda kissed her boyfriend on the cheek.
6. Three men bought an expensive car from a dishonest dealer.
7. A hungry man ate a sandwich in one minute.
8. Professor Morandi is a patient person.
9. My sister met her boyfriend on the bus going to Philadelphia.
10. My favorite book is *Love in the Time of Cholera*.
11. Her red house is located near a hazardous waste dump, but she loves it.
12. In the summer, boys always look at girls on the beach.
13. The black and white photograph at the end of the chapter is interesting.

UNIT 9: PASSIVE VOICE
Activity 9-1 (page 138)
1. A I lost the necklace yesterday. **The necklace was lost yesterday.**
2. P The man was found "not guilty."
3. A Civil war has affected many countries. **Many countries have been affected by civil war.**
4. A Rik is firing Alma this week. **Alma is being fired by Rik this week.**
5. A Pine Grove police officers will catch the thief. **The thief will be caught by Pine Grove police officers.**
6. P Fourteen people were hurt in the bus accident.
7. A The storm cut power to the whole town. **Power to the whole town was cut by the storm.**
8. A The principal will give both girls a warning about their behavior. **Both girls will be given a warning about their behavior by the principal.**

Activity 9-4 (page 141)
1 were elected.
2 is used
3 is reached
4 is granted
5 is give
6 are needed
7 were contested
8 were surprised
9 were punched
10 was argued
11 was awarded
12 were added
13 will be chosen.

Activity 9-6 (page 143)
1. Thanksgiving was started by the Pilgrims many years ago.
2. NO CHANGE Thanksgiving is an important holiday in the United States.
3. On Thanksgiving, a big parade is held by New York City.
4. Turkeys will be cooked by many American families.
5. NO CHANGE I will go to my friend's house for Thanksgiving.
6. A lot of food will be bought by people for the holiday.
7. Meals will be served to homeless people by students.
8. A talk will be given on the radio by the president.
9. A big party was given by my family last year.
10. School will be closed for the next two days.

Activity 9-8 (page 145)
A.
1. The boring movie made the entire audience yawn.
2. The amazed audience didn't move an inch during the performance.
3. Their disappointed teacher told them to stay after class.
4. The best seller wasn't a very interesting novel.
5. That annoying little boy won't stop screaming.
6. The surprising news left everyone shocked.
7. She wanted to pet my sleeping dog.
8. Computerized translators will work better in the future.